BAR
PINOTXO

GOD IS IN
THE GARBANZOS

Robin Willis

Art Direction and Design: Enric Jardi
Photography: Becky Lawton
Edited by Mike Gust

Barcelona
www.hotpotato.press
info@hotpotato.press

Copyright © 2016 Robin Willis

First edition: October 2016

Book Production by Núria Garcia
at I am Núria.

ISBN: 978-84-608-6811-8

Impreso en España / Printed in Spain

To Zoe, my quadrilingual daughter, who has
from the very beginning preferred *pa amb
tomàquet* to Big Macs. And to Montse
López Garcia, who could find bliss in
a grilled ham and cheese sandwich,
a Coca Cola and a Johnny Cash tune.

"UN PAÍS POBRE TIENE UNA COCINA RICA."

Jordi Asín

TABLE of CONTENTS

INTRODUCTION, 11
Foreword by John Gorham, **12**
Foreword by Carme Ruscalleda, **14**
A Word about Words, **16**
The Method to This Madness, **17**
Acknowledgements, **18**
Per què? **20**

THE PLACE, 31
Pinotxo? **32**
All about Albert, **33**
Work and Home, **35**
Ánimo, **36**
Temporada, **37**
A Tale of Two Teams, **38**
The Show Must Go On, **39**

OYE, CATERINA! 41
Early Days, **42**
It Wasn't Fireworks, **44**
Food, **48**
Pinotxo 2.0, **49**
Running and the Olympics, **53**
Award Night, **55**
María, **57**

THE PEOPLE, 59
Juanito, **60**
Jordi, **62**
María José, **63**
Albert, Dídac, Daniel, Javi, Esther and Olivia, **64-65**

PROVISIONS, 67

RECIPES, 71
Samfaina, **72**
Pa amb tomàquet, **74**
Sofregit, **78**
Picada, **80**
All i oli, **84**
Romesco, **88**
Estofat de vedella, **90**
Reduction of balsamic vinegar, **93**
Calamarsets saltats amb fesols de Santa Pau, **94**
Truita de bacallà, **96**
Empedrat de llenties amb bacallà, **100**
Tonyina escabetxada, **104**
Faves a la catalana, **108**
Remenat de tallarines, **110**
Remenat de gambes, **113**
Peking duck, **114**

Cigrons amb botifarra negra i ceba, **118**
Pollastre a la catalana, **120**
Fricandó amb moxernons, **122**
Suquet de rap, **124**
Bacallà amb ceba i pebrot verd confitats, **128**
Trinxat de la Cerdanya, **132**
Fideuà rossejat, **134**
Arroz caldoso con pollo y setas, **139**
Rabo de toro, **141**
Musclos amb ceba i tomàquet, **146**
Escalivada, **148**
Jordi's Saturday morning egg, **152**
Gambas a la plancha, **156**

POSTRES, 161
Manzanas al horno, **162**
Croissant azucarado, **164**

SALIDAS & ADÉU, 165

PHOTO CREDITS, 168

TRICKS, TRUCOS, ESSAYS, AND SIDES

El secret del tomàquet beneït, **76**

Duende, **82**

Small Plates: The Mystery of the Esmorzars de Forquilla, **87**

Volcano Beans, **94**

Baca... what?, **98**

El Rebost: Cuina de llauna i cosas secas, **102**

What's in a Pot, **107**

For a Few Ollas More, **117**

Ode to a Friedora, **127**

The Problem with Peppers, **131**

It's the Caldo, **136**

Go Soak Your Beans, **144**

Braise Moi, **150**

A la plancha, **155**

Iberian Eating, **158**

INTRODUCTION

JOHN GORHAM

John Gorham is owner and executive chef of the iconic Portland, Oregon restaurants Toro Bravo, Tasty n Sons, Tasty n Alder, Plaza del Toro, and co-owner of the Mediterranean Exploration Company, Pollo Bravo and Shalom Ya'll.

Truth be told, John's ceaseless hard work, taste, generosity, cooking chops, and passion has contributed so much to Portland's reputation as one of the world's best culinary cities. His boundless curiosity, good nature, and love of what he does infuses everything he touches.

"AS I APPROACHED THE BAR, I REALIZED THIS PLACE I REVERE SO HIGHLY REPRESENTS THE EPICENTER OF MY LOVE FOR THIS ENTIRE INDUSTRY."

It is with both great pride and humility that I write this foreword for one of the most inspirational restaurants I have encountered in my lifetime. I felt it was such an honor to be asked that I had to make the trip back to Barcelona to find the words that would properly portray my respect for Pinotxo.

As I approached the bar, I realized this place I revere so highly represents the epicenter of my love for this entire industry. The love of the craft is felt the moment you step up to the bar. Pinotxo embodies so many of the beliefs that I think it takes to run successful restaurants. The hospitality you'll receive transcends time. With each passed plate, every bite and sip, I fall more in love with this place. My perspective of genuine hospitality broadens with each visit. For locals and visitors alike Pinotxo represents **SPANISH EPICUREAN CULTURE**, one snail at a time. I don't believe there is another restaurant that better illustrates the versatile cuisine Spain has to offer.

Bar Pinotxo is the first culinary experience for so many who make the voyage to Barcelona, as I did 10 years ago. Pinotxo is always my first stop. It's my meet back place when I bring friends and family to the market. When I travel, I seek out the best of the best. My quest for the perfect chipirones, cockles, or botifarra always leads me back to where it all started. Pinotxo is both as local as it gets and one of the best destination restaurant in the world. For me it is the fulcrum of **MY FAVORITE FOOD CITY IN THE WORLD: BARCELONA!**

Pinotxo has been thriving for over 60 years now, by bringing 'farm to table' to their guests long before it was a voiced concept. The bar still gets mad respect, year after year. As it is truly an institution, I wasn't at all surprised when Juanito Bayén was named by the city of Barcelona as the restaurateur of the year. That's right, Juanito is the gentleman in the bow tie who just made you the best cortado you've ever had. His seasoned professionalism and unobtrusive quality service casually bridges the chaos of the market and Pinotxo's identity: a true bar de mercado. No question; this is as authentic as it gets.

The definition of a family affair, Jordi Asín, Juanito's nephew, mans the stoves while María José, wife of Jordi, and their son, Luka, will be there to serve you. Ask for a business card and you'll get handed a plaque from the top of a Cava bottle with an ancient picture of the family from a lifetime ago. Look closely and you'll see a young kid who just happens to be a much younger version of the bowtied gentleman who just passed you a plate of their famous **GARBANZOS WITH MORCILLA**.

I can assure you that no one else in the world is more excited than myself that this family is about to share their secret recipes, love of food, and stories found within the pages of this cookbook as they have shaped my entire culinary career. Bar Pinotxo is at the center of my gastronomic universe.

CARME RUSCALLEDA

F or those of us who have turned food into an essential element in our way of living, feeling, and behaving, *mercados* are the calling card of a city. Barcelona enjoys an amazing network of municipal markets, which are currently being restored and modernized. These institutions constitute a fantastic cultural heritage and offer an extraordinary variety of fresh products of the highest quality to both consumers and cooking professionals.

La Boqueria is a must-see visit in Barcelona, and those who discover it for the first time immediately realize that La Boqueria is much more than a market: its location, its architecture, the eclectic sum of its stalls and displayed items; they all make La Boqueria a space which seduces everyone.

Passing the beautiful portico of the main entrance, you find, to the right, the marquee and the awning that flaunts the brand of one of the most desired gourmet icons of the city of Barcelona, Joan (Juanito to everybody!) Bayén's **BAR PINOTXO**, a place that overflows with sympathy, vitality, complicity, agility, and service at the bar, seducing both local and foreign clientele. Because, well, at **PINOTXO BAR**, Juanito knows how to thrill gourmets, making them feel each morning the positive pleasure of the message in Joan Manuel Serrat's song, "Hoy puede ser un gran día" (Today can be a great day).

Though Juanito likes to introduce his bar as "un chiringuito en el mercado" (a beach bar at the market), behind his rascal smirk he knows very well that **PINOTXO BAR** enjoys a success without rival, with the city at its feet and the recently awarded Premio de Gastronomia Ciudad de Barcelona (The City of Barcelona Gastronomy Prize).

The gourmet seduction is served: take your seat at the bar, be happy at **BAR PINOTXO** in La Boqueria and take home this genius cookbook, guaranteed by Juanito and the crew of Bar Pinotxo!

Let this be known, Carme Ruscalleda is the only woman chef in the world with five Michelin stars. Let that sink in for a minute. 5 Michelin stars. Sant Pau, her restaurant in the lovely seaside village of Sant Pol de Mar, just up the coast from Barcelona, has year in and year out distilled the magic of Catalan cuisine into elegant, heartfelt, always evolving dishes that somehow capture the essence and character of this stunningly beautiful and bountiful region. Her other Michelin starred restaurant in Tokyo and her presence as the executive chef for Moments Restaurant at Barcelona's Mandarin Oriental Hotel only add to her reputation as one the world's best chefs.

"LA BOQUERIA'S EL PINOTXO, THE CITY OF BARCELONA'S GOURMET ICON"

A WORD ABOUT WORDS

Let's face it, my Spanish *es* très, très *mal*. I speak like a monkey. OK, perhaps an adorable monkey but a monkey nonetheless. People say things like, "**OH THAT'S ALRIGHT; YOU JUST GOT HERE**." No, I haven't. It's going on fifteen years now. Also, it's not called "**SPANISH**" in Catalunya (and much of Latin America). It's called Castellano. The thinking is that Spain is a place and not a language. OK?

So know this. I'm not a savant when it comes to languages. My daughter, on the other hand, speaks four languages with absolute, dead-on fluency. The Dad? Nope. "**AH**" talk *El castellano de monos* (monkeys).... And Catalan? "**MOLT BÉ!**" (mohl behh). "**SI US PLAU.**" (see oos PLOW).

THE METHOD TO THIS MADNESS

I have basically followed the custom of kitchens around the world, which is to adopt whatever language is handy.

Throughout this book you will find words in both Castellano and Catalan. Sometimes I translate them into English and sometimes I don't. I know there is a reason for this but I can't quite articulate it. Maybe I am trying to put you, the reader, back behind that twenty-five foot bar... dodging butts and hovering over the flat top, flipping gambas, and feeding coffee orders to Juanito at just the right interval. It's an *escudella barrejada* (mixed stew) of cooking, listening, dancing and occasionally wrestling, all greased by a myriad of languages issuing forth from both the *equipo* and the customers. Have your dictionary handy and rest assured that if something is in any way life-threatening or has the potential of bursting into flames I have tried to spell it out for you. *Molt bé!*

ACKNOWLEDGEMENTS

From wandering in to Pinotxo two years ago in an attempt to jump start my slightly worse for wear love affair with Spain, Catalunya, and Barcelona, to impersonating a missing in action Hawaiian wine buyer at the region's oldest and very much hidden factoria de *vermut*, the making of this book has been quite a ride. I have had lots of help steering good ship, "**BAR PINOTXO: GOD IS IN THE GARBANZOS.**"

Besides offering moral support, creative collaboration, playlist sharing, access to the inner circle of the Catalan publishing empire, and leading this production away from design mundanity and into something truly remarkable, Enic Jardí not only served as art director and book designer, he also conducted the interviews with all of the people who don't speak my native language. This would be everybody. *Gràcies, amic.*

As the project went from weeks, to months, to... oh never mind... Enric brought in Noël Yebra and Ignasi Portales to add needed focus and, generally, allow him to hide from me. We both thank you.

Considering my desire to be the Hunter S. Thompson... make that the Ralph Steadman, of culinary prose, I can't say enough good things about my old friend and brilliant writer, Mike Gust, who somehow... was able to... make sense of my unique way with punctuation... tense... and; sentence structure. Beyond fixing the grammatical nuts and bolts of this production he offered, reason, moral support, a shoulder to cry on, and if memory serves, an absolutely delicious turkey sandwich while we were esconced in the final read through.

Becky Lawton's photography for the gorgeous *Cuina* magazine has undoubtedly contributed to Barcelona being one of the world's great food hubs. This same elegant and delicious photography has certainly lifted the quality of this humble endeavor into the big leagues. And Bjorn Badetti, our resident Swedish-Italian, has kept the chow looking both real and real tasty with his subtle retouching.

Keeping it real, my culinary police force included two of the best cooks I know: Suzi Conklin and Sasha Kaplan. Suzi's been picking me up and dusting me off for decades, and Sasha's support and always optimistic spin on life's real treasures (brownies, apricot jam making, family, and the inherent beauty in seasonal garden maintenance) has allowed me to focus on the flowers and not the weeds.

Considering my ongoing lack of facility with other languages, I must acknowledge the help of Marta Maurel, Andres Quintero, and Maria Gasol Boncompte, who saved my life translating interviews, stories, and snippets (in both Catalan and Castellano) into something I could get my addled brain around.

A last minute "Hail Mary" was performed by Mercè Bayén Garcia who came to the rescue with the motherlode of Clan Pinotxo family photos. *Molt bé, Mercè!*

Benedicte Bodard has been there from day one, pushing, prodding, and gnawing, using a combination of encouragement, bribes, and extortion to get me to get this sucker done. *Merci. Merci. Merci.*

A big hug to Mario Scattoloni for finding his great shots of Señor Adrià, as well as his ability to capture the color and craziness of the Boqueria and las Ramblas.

Thank you, Alfonso Beato, for manning the video camera during the many interviews. And *saludos a* Kike for standing in for Alfonso when he couldn't make it.

Lots of thanks to my resident *experto en carne*, Esteve Fosalba Moya, who taught me more than I really wanted to know about *nervios, tendones, grasas intramusculares*, etc. Seriously, here in España, the only difference between a surgeon and a great *carnicero* is that in the former the patient gets diagnosed and in the latter they get turned into a roast. Sorry.

Gràcies to all my *amics* in the *mercats* who have graciously suffered through my endless questions and "monkey" *Castellano*, with big smiles, generosity with nary a raised eyebrow.

Thanks also to my friends and family for their constant inquiries regarding the book's completion date. It has motivated me to "get'r done" to honor their care and support, and yeah... to get them to stop asking.

A big shout out to the Portland, Oregon contingent; John and Renee Gorham and company, and Liz Crain, who somehow appeared well into the game and contributed much guidance and encouragement.

Cristina Jolonch, the food editor at Barcelona's major daily La Vanguardia, was ever so helpful in making introductions with the local guild of *cocineros extrodinarios*.

Also regarding historic photos, *moltíssimes gràcies* to Conxi Petit at the Arxiu Nacional de Catalunya (The National Archive of Catalunya).

Riding herd on all the printing and production minutia was Núria Garcia. *Salut!*

Of course none of this would have been possible without Jordi, María Jose, Juanito, and the *equipo* of Bar Pinotxo. *"Té calamarsets amb fesols de Santa Pau?"*

And finally to the people of Catalunya, Galicia, Asturias, Euskadi, Andalucía, Castilla y León, Castilla-La Mancha, Extremadura, Madrid, Aragón, Valencia, Murcia, Cantabria, Rioja, and of course Navarra, all of whom at this point, still make up España, my beloved adopted homeland, *un embarazada fuego.*

When I brought my family to Barcelona many years ago we explored the city in the usual ways. The Pedrera. Casa Batlló. Getting purposely lost in the plazas of the Barrio de Gràcia. Getting unpurposely lost in the Barrio Gótico. The Sagrada Família at dawn. The Sagrada Família at dusk. The Sagrada Família at noon. The chapel under the Sagrada Família. The towers of the Sagrada Família… they used to let you climb them then. The Cathedral and the *abuelas* and *abuelos* dancing the Sardana in front of the Cathedral and the pile of coats in the middle of the Sardana in front of the Cathedral watched over by the dancing *abuelas* and the *abuelos* who would get excited and let go with a "**WHOO-HOO!**" when the *cobla* (the traditional, sometimes squeaky sounding orchestra that accompanies the dancers) would crank up the volume just a notch.

Of course, we sauntered down the (pre-Pakistanis selling their glow in the dark helicopter thingies and bird whistles) Las Ramblas and the *paradas* (stands) selling flowers and chipmunks, canaries and chickens, mice and lizards, past the human statues, and the shell games and the pickpockets circling the shills, and the marks watching the shell games. And then the 8th wonder of the food world… **THE BOQUERIA**.

Back where I come from, fresh fish, more or less, still comes in a plastic wrapped styrofoam tray and is called either surmi (AKA "**KRAZY KRAB**"), salmon or "**RED SNAPPER**"… with "**RED SNAPPER**" standing in pretty much for anything that isn't salmon. Here in the Boqueria there was salmon and… salmonettes, *rape* (monkfish) that looked like a cross between Edward G. Robinson and Peter Lorre towards the end of his career, sad but vicious looking **MERLUZA, DORADO, LENGUADO, ADULT SEPIA, ADOLESCENT SEPIA, BABY SEPIA… CHIPIRONES, BACALAO… ESQUEIXADA (SHREDDED), SOAKED OR DRY AS A CHUNK OF GRANITE, IN BUÑUELOS… CALAMARI, ATÚN, MERO, EMPERADOR, LUBINA, ARENQUES, SARDINAS, BUEY DE MAR, NÉCORAS, BOGAVANTES, TALLERINAS, MEJILLONES, AND SEEMINGLY TEN OTHER KINDS OF ALMEJAS, OSTRAS, GAMBAS…** big ones from South America, and smaller, redder, and really expensive ones from just up the coast in Palamós… **CIGALAS, NAVAJAS, HÍGADO DE RAPE, RASCA, PULPO, PULPITOS, PERCEBES…** most of them whole, most of them with their heads on and looking at you, and some with their heads on and still kicking. There were bags of snails and piles of entrails, white fluffy tripe bath towels, tongues that invariably had tales to tell to the piles of ears which were listening for the magic phrase, "**Y CUATRO OREJAS Y UN MORRO PARA NO ESTAR SOLO… ÉSTE, ES MUY GUAPO.**" And speaking of tales… of course they had tails… *toro, vaca y cerdo*. And rabbits dressed in their fur coats, hanging bat-like by their feet.

The frontline of paradas were dug in to counter the waves of snapping, drawling, pushing, gaping tourists, all speaking in a tidal wave of different languages, but seemingly not one word of "**SPANISH**" or, God forbid… "**WHAT… THEY SPEAK ANOTHER LANGUAGE HERE!?**" CATALAN? OK, maybe an "**HOLA**" or "**SÍ**" or a "**GRA-THEE-ATH**" but the torrent of questions like "**WHAT IS THAT THING WITH A HOOF?**" or "**HOW MUCH IS THAT IN DOLLARS, MARKS, POUNDS, YEN, KRONER, BAT?**" were delivered just like they were talking to the checker at Ralph's, Tesco, Penny Markt, or Monoprix.

Just off to the right, and thronged by a huge mass of people, was tiny Bar Pinotxo, where at the prow stood a short, wiry "**WELL PRESERVED**" guy enthusiastically greeting customers, pouring cava and beer, making tri-level coffees, helping the newbies into plates of *gambas*, doing the cuenta on a tiny, narrow pad of paper, and cycling the happy diners on and off of their stools in record time. We newly arrived *guiri's* (AKA non Iberian, AKA pink person from el norte) assumed this whirlwind of smiles and commerce must be the namesake and owner of the joint. It must be the famous, "**SEÑOR PINOTXO**" no doubt. "**BON DIA! I HAVE FRESCH SHRIMPS FROM PALAMÓS AND ALMEJAS TOO-DAY! WE COOK FOR YOU! OK? SIÉNTESE.**"

As the years passed, I grew jaded with the Ramblas and the Boqueria. I found my shopping home at other *mercados* and yep... the "**SUPER**." As beautiful as it was, the Ramblas was for *estranjero* rubes looking for giant beers, buckets of Sangría, "**OK PAELLA**", Mexican *sombreros,* and Barça jerseys. Obviously, the Mossos (Catalan storm troopers) were in on the shell game. The Boqueria was a trap for suckers looking for "**JAMÓN SERRANO ESPAÑOL**" and *zumos* (fruit juice) that got cheaper and less watery the farther you dove into that great beautiful barn.

I peppered my visiting foreign friends with dire warnings, explaining that the best place for your passport was in the nightstand, and if you had to take a day pack, it should be slung in front with both of your arms clamped firmly over it. Wallets should be stowed securely in the left front pocket with the owner's hand clamped firmly on top of it, and should only contain enough cash for immediate purchases. All plastic belonged at home with the passport. *Cuidado!!!*

Still, even in the deepest depths of my world-weary expat "**LIFER**" role, I knew it was all just a ruse. I had seen the Ramblas at dawn. I had watched the crew of Pinotxo quietly and graciously accommodate a six deep gaggle of confused and anxious putzfraus, notebook toting foodies, pushy investment bankers with their trophy brides, nintendo wielding picky niños looking for mcnuggets, still drunk lobster red lager louts and lout-ettes, Frenchies looking for waiters and tables and more silverware, Taiwanese salesmen ready to go to the mat over the freshness of the *mariscos,* and of course the local regulars... all while simultaneously dodging butts in a kitchen that would not be inappropriate in a medium sized Winnebago. And yet somehow they had time to steer a nice, older couple from Des Moines away from their neighbor's *callos* (tripe) and into *lo mejor del mejor estofado,* or the simple but brilliant *garbanzos con morcilla y cebollas,* or to a single egg, fried to perfection, served atop a couple slices of God's own pancetta and a few crispy hand carved slivers of potatoes.

MY CYNICISM WAS A SHAM

Like with just about everything in Spain and Catalunya, I was in love. And like everything in Spain and Catalunya it was both simple and complicated. And really, was paying one or two euros for a watery *zumo* that much of a surcharge for *lo mejor del mejor mercado en todo el mundo*? It was time to rekindle the affair. **IT WAS TIME FOR BAR PINOTXO TO TAKE ME HOME**.

The opportunity arose as most opportunities arise, by following a whim... or was that a hunch? Let's just call it happenstance. I had the chance to house sit at a magnificent *piso* for a week in what some consider to be Barcelona's most dodgy neighborhood, the Raval. Let them consider it so and stay away. For me the Raval is the beating heart of the city.

I truly did want to revise my opinion of the Boqueria. As the aforementioned Bar Pinotxo was just a block away from the flat, I hatched a plan. Each day I would visit the Boqueria and have lunch at Pinotxo, where "**ONE PLATE AT A TIME**", I would divine a new appreciation for this often tourist-battered part of town.

It was time to implement phase one. Looking for authenticity, I entered the Boqueria from the side the tourists never see... the *culo*... The ass... back by the giant, *apestoso* industrial trash compactors. I passed by the famous "**PETRÀS BOLETS**" *parada* featuring seemingly every non-hallucinogenic fungus known to mankind... and maybe a few hallucinogenic ones if you ask them nicely.

I pushed on and into the inner fish circle. Like some sort of hell for aquatic animals, the Boqueria's fish section is set up in concentric rings with the stands for *mariscos, bacalao,* and other preserved fish on the outside, and an unbelievable number of fresh fish folks glaring at each other on the inside. I then moved through the **ZONA DE OFFAL**... five stands selling nothing but innards, variety meats, *menuts*... guts. God bless you Iberians and your desire to use up every bit of *animales* but is there really that big of a market for tongues, brains, stomachs, lymph glands and testicles? I am, in general, an adventurous eater, but not once in my life have I ever shot straight up in bed at three in the morning with an insatiable desire to consume a pig's colon.

Eventually, I arrived at the Boqueria's frontline and my destination: Bar Pinotxo. It was as hopping as usual but I was able to plop down on a stool that had miraculously just been vacated. I took this to be a good omen. The Pinotxo crew was in fine balletic form, bobbing and weaving to match the rhythms of orders, and calmly helping the patrons decide on what to have for lunch.

Confession... For as long as I remember I have been staring at other people's plates of food. Some people gaze into their partner's eyes, watch birds, planes and/or various attractive and unattractive people and their various attractive and unattractive body parts. I, on the other hand, stare at meals belonging to complete strangers. On my right a young couple was sharing an order of *garbanzos* and *morcilla* and washing it down with *cava*... on the left a couple of Asian ladies were

having a beautiful brown and gooey *estofado* and a whack of baby squids... AKA *chipirones*... AKA *calamarsets*. My gaze shifted from the pile of tiny loligo vulgaris to the big brown soulful eyes and wry smile of the waitress (whom I would find out later was named María José) and who had guessed that this would be what I was having.

I placed my order and within moments I was looking at a plate of cephalopoda *niños y niñas* snatched from the prime of their lives. Snatched or not, all those lightly sauteed tiny completely intact bodies looked incredibly tasty. The squidlets had been laid to rest on a mound of tiny white beans. Hmmm... could these be the famous?... **"FESOLS DE SANTA PAU!"** These words shot out of my mouth as if I had some rare form of Tourettes that caused me to uncontrollably shout names of exotic legumes. Suddenly, seven heads seemingly turned as one from their stations at the *plancha*, the Pilsner Urquel tap, the espresso machine, and, if memory serves, the dishwasher. It was like in that ancient Groucho Marx TV show "**YOU BET YOUR LIFE**" ,where, if during the introductory chat, a contest would say **THE MAGIC WORD** a model T horn would go off and a rubber duck on a string would drop down, signaling that the contestant had won a set of steak knives or a bath mat. Apparently ,"*Fesols de Santa Pau*" was the magic phrase.

Although no rubber duck dropped from the ceiling, I had instead triggered much staring, gesturing, and whispering from behind the counter. The tribunal conferred and made their decision. Jordi, a thin, angularly good looking and prematurely gray haired guy (whose name I discovered thanks to it being

embroidered on his chef's jacket), and who had been working the plancha and the fogons, looked me in the eye and asked, **"WHAT ARE YOU DOING TOMORROW MORNING?"** I looked over at María José. She was doing that wry smile thing again. **"UH... WELL... WHAT TIME?"**, I said, trying to figure out just what I was getting myself into.

"**6:30... YOU AND I WILL OPEN UP AND THEN I'LL SHOW YOU HOW TO MAKE A COUPLE OF THINGS.**"

Without missing a beat, I said, **"OK. I'M IN."** María José nodded her head as Jordi turned back to rescue the *almejas* from under the upturned pyrex bread *pan*. I seemed to be levitating a few inches above my bar stool. The die was cast. I was going to help open the world renowned **BAR PINOTXO.**

The first day of my new life as Jordi Asín's prep boy began with a tour of the predawn Boqueria. Shhhhh... there are two Barcelonas. Version One is crazy busy, sometimes stinky, way too crowded with too many people from God knows where eating *muy auténtico* **TAPAS** and **OK PAELLA**, washed down with Don Simon Sangria.

The other Barcelona is darkly *romàntic, tranquil,* mysterious, peaceful, bucolic, song bird-infused, and drenched with a half-light that makes you want to buy a ukulele and sing the Israel Kamakawiwo'ole's version of "**WHAT A WONDERFUL WORLD**", and just a heck of a long way from Main Street, USA. It is also available only between the hours of five to seven in the morning... so if you're visiting, get yo booty out of bed early and enjoy it. I do... and did particularly on that chilly November morning.

At slightly before six I descended the stairs of the flat. Except for the *panaderia* opening up, I had all of Carrer Hospital to myself. I headed up the narrow and seemingly medieval, *Carrer de la Petxina*... which is this really beautiful sort of secret passage entering the Boqueria, which is neither as unceremonious nor as odoriferous as the back end, or as horrifically touristy as the front end just off the Ramblas... which as mentioned previously, at this time of day, was neither of those things. What it was, was... all mine.

I made my way past the closed-up *paradas*... **EL HOGAR DEL POLLO QUILI**, **MENUTS JAVIER**, **TOCINERÍA VÍCTOR I PAQUITA**, **FRUITES I VERDURES CAL NEGUIT**. All was quiet now... their metal gates drawn while they savored their last moments of sleep before all hell broke loose. I rounded the bend to see that Jordi had just arrived and was beginning his morning rituals. We exchanged sleepy but warm *bon dias* and I hopped right in, ready to do my best on my first day.

Institutions like Pinotxo really are living things... and as such, can, if need be, repel invading microbes like me. It's best to take things a little slowly at first... to stand back and look and ask before you say... reprogram the cash register. I was intent on dodging Pinotxo's immune system.

The early morning regulars were arriving and Jordi was preparing the first rounds of *café con leche* and *cortados*. After one of the members of the Pinotxo breakfast club showed me how to set up the long-legged exterior tables "**JUST SO**", I headed over to see if I could mess up anything in the kitchen. Observing maritime and kitchen protocol, I requested to come aboard the good ship Pinotxo.

Let me state the obvious... the kitchen of Pinotxo is unbelievably tiny. It's a submarine's galley. It's a tunnel; a small tube of culinary wonder. It's dinky! It's not like they just use the place for a final prep and a pass through the microwave... everything... and I mean everything... over one thousand meals a week... comes out of a space that is about the dimensions of a "**STREET OF DREAMS**" walk-in closet.

Jordi asked me what I wanted to learn how to cook. I explained that I was here to help, to do menial labor... to be a galley slave. He acknowledged my commitment and then said we needed to whup up the first round of their famous *garbanzos* with *morcilla*. But first we needed the *morcilla*. Jordi asked me to run to a specific *parada* and bring back the required blood sausage.

RIGHT! OK! MORCILLA! YES SIR! YOU WANT MORCILLA? YOU WILL HAVE MORCILLA.

I flew out of the kitchen and followed Jordi's directions to the letter. "**TO THE LEFT, TWO AISLES OVER AND ONE AISLE DOWN. THE LITTLE CANSALADERIA ON THE END. TELL HER YOU ARE FROM PINOTXO.**" Within seconds I arrived at the little *cansaladeria* on the end. It was shut up as tight as a can of anchovies de Cantabria. *Joder*... Should I show initiative and do the eager beaver, knucklehead thing and find the *morcilla* someplace else? "**HEY LOOK... COACH THEY DIDN'T HAVE THE MORCILLA BUT I GOT YOU A ZUCCHINI INSTEAD!**" Nah, I reported back sausageless.

"**NO PROBLEM...**" I was getting the feeling that not much was a problem for Jordi... I mean serving a thousand diners a week, all of whom were looking for their defining culinary moment in **BARTHELONA**; from a chicken coop-sized metal box filled with flames, seven dancing butts connected to seven distinct and complex personalities, twelve hours a day, six days a week, eleven months out of the year, probably keeps things like temporarily missing morcilla in perspective.

Jordi moved me on to *cap-i-pota* (head and foot). Now the first thing you need to know about *cap-i-pota* is that, in its modern version, it is only *cap* and no *pota*. So what exactly is *cap*... Brains? No. Cheek? No. Tongue. No.... *Cap* is... wait for it... pig face. Yes... that's right. Morro... *Cara* de Porky Pig. I don't know why the occasional facial transplant holds such a fascination for the rest of the world but at the boqueria there are paradas with pig faces stacked upon pig faces. Happy ones. Sad ones. Grumpy ones. Laughing ones. Luckily, the pig face I was dealing with had been cut into unrecognizable chunks which I stirred around and around in a big pot. While I was dealing with Porky's mug, Jordi had snuck out and returned with the morcilla. Either the shop had just opened or I had been waiting in front of **ESTHER AND MONTSE'S BACALAO AND MORE** and didn't know it.

Jordi gently issued the instructions for the *garbanzos* and I dove right in to my newest chore. I took a couple of *morcillas*, removed their casings, and then cut them into big chunks. Then I squirted some olive oil in a pan, and added the *morcilla* and commenced to busting it up with a wooden spoon. After a while I added a whack of caramelized onions that a thoughtful someone had prepared beforehand. When everything was nicely cooked through I emptied a tupperware container's worth of nice fat *garbanzos* into the *pan*, gave them gentle stir, then placed the empty container on the handy metal counter next to the stove. Jordi reappeared, complimented me on my kitchen prowess, and then discreetly scraped melted plastic off the cover of what turned out to be, not a countertop, but a flat grill.

At this point the real crew arrived and as they began to fill up the walk-in closet of a kitchen, I decided this might be a good time to end my first day. As hearty hand clasps were exchanged and backs were slapped, I made a promise to come back for lunch to taste the fruits of our labor.

I returned that afternoon, ordered the garbanzos, then screwed up my courage for the *cap-i-pota*. Jordi brought the *garbanzos* which were and always are delicious. As he took the empty plate he delivered the sad news that the *cap-i-pota* was no more... finito... *acabado*... sold out. He suggested the *callos* as a substitute. I looked him in the eye and said... "**BRING IT JEFE. BRING IT.**"

Since my stay in the Raval, I've returned to Pinotxo many times, and it was during these many visits that the idea for this book was hatched, fried and put on a plate...

Hey look! The nice, older couple from Des Moines are leaving... grab a stool. We're in!

THE PLACE

PINOTXO?

JORDI: "Some people think that Juanito is Pinotxo but it's not true. Pinotxo was a dog that belonged to my mother and Juanito when they were children and his name came from the Disney movie that had just been released. He did this trick where you give him a thousand peseta bill and tell him to go get change and he'd run off and come back with ten, one-hundred peseta bills. Everyday he came to the bar with my mother and at that time none of the paradas had names, they just had numbers. Everybody loved him and would say "hey let's go to the bar with that little dog, Pinotxo." So one thing led to another and the bar became known as Pinotxo's Bar... Bar Pinotxo."

THIS IS NOT "THE" DOG PINOTXO, BUT IT IS A DOG AT PINOTXO.

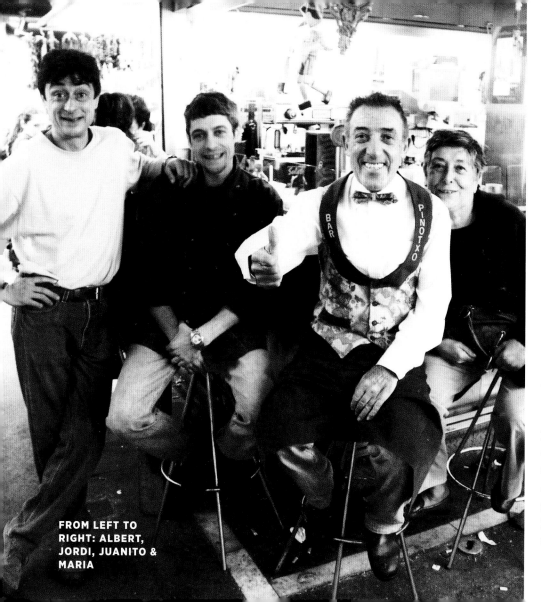

FROM LEFT TO RIGHT: ALBERT, JORDI, JUANITO & MARIA

ALL ABOUT
ALBERT

Jordi's brother, Albert died of leukemia in 02011. It was Albert who guided the kitchen through "**EL BOOM**", the exciting but not exactly easy years of the 1992 Olympics. Albert opened up the menu to reflect his interests in the tastes from around the world. His gregarious personality kept the crew centered, motivated, and happy. Like Jordi says: **"THE GOOD THING IS THAT NO ONE IS INDISPENSABLE BUT THE BAD THING IS THAT NO ONE IS INDIS-PENSABLE. THE BAR STAYS OPEN."**

How does a space no bigger than a walk-in closet deal with such a loss? This "**JUST GET ON WITH IT**" spirit of the inhabitants of my adopted country is one of the things I am most charmed by. It's not indifference… it's not a lack of care… it's just that life goes on and there's a lot of work still to do and

33

more life to live. In the following passages Jordi and María José add some perspective.

JORDI: Like all of us, the bar was part of Albert's life from a very young age. Our family has always been in touch with food and cooking and it is really part of our lives. Albert took it very seriously and I guess he began in earnest around 1988 when he was thirty-two.

Before that he studied pharmacology, but he gave that up and started working in wholesale fish and then later he sold wines and then in sales for a multinational.

MARÍA JOSÉ: He was kind of restless. He was curious.

J: But then he came back to the bar and he loved it; he loved cooking. He changed the menu... From "classics" to "new dishes." He tasted and tested things.

MJ: Yes, that was Albert.

J: One of his "new" dishes was *garbanzos* and *morcilla*. It's a typical dish here. *Garbanzos* and *morcilla* with onions and local herbs. But my brother liked flavors from other cultures. His version included *chimichurri*, an Argentinian herb and spice mixture. So he combined these flavors with local things like *garbanzos*, caramelized onions, and of course *morcilla*. Lots of places have this on the menu but ours is unique because of Albert's sensitivity and innovation.

MJ: He was always experimenting in his lab, tasting and testing things. He loved the feel, the smell and of course the taste of things. He was always working on something and he'd invite us all to have a taste.

J: It also was like this at home. Besides being cooks, we have always gone out to try things and watch other cooks. Albert loved this. We'd go to Thai and Indian restaurants and then we'd try to figure out how they did it. Even now, as a family of five, when we go to a new restaurant we order five different things. You never know what you will get. We taste everything and then we compare. Then we try to figure out how they made it. It's a very important process for us.

MJ: Then we try to make it at home.

J: It's not for the bar. It's just pure curiosity. You can continue to do things the same way or you can shake things up.

MJ: Albert liked to cook snails too. He had a girlfriend in Lleida and her Grandmother gave him a recipe.

J: It's the same recipe we use at the bar now. They are prepared with a salsa seca... almonds and sausage. It's typical of Lleida. You know, a little spicy.

MJ: And he loved to cook *rabo de toro* too. You know he was not born to be a cook. He didn't study for it but he had the ability and he liked it.

J: Before Albert, the bar never served rabo but Albert said, "I have to cook *rabo*, I have to!"

WORK AND HOME

MARÍA JOSÉ
I leave a little bit earlier than Jordi. When he comes home I usually ask him how he felt things went. Other than that we usually don't speak about work or the market or anything related to it.

JORDI
The work in the bar can be stressful, really stressful; there are lots of people and noise during the entire day. When you get home it's time for a change.

MJ: You become aware of the noise and stress only when you stop. When you are at the bar you really only can focus on the work.

J: When you are right in the middle of it you don't realize it but when you get home and stop...

MJ: Jordi's responsible for everything. What the the daily special is, when we change the menu... everything.

ÁNIMO

MARÍA JOSÉ: Albert had this curiosity. He traveled too.

JORDI: He went to India.

MARÍA: And he always traveled alone.

J: He said that by traveling by himself he was able to learn things and get closer to the people.

He went to Kashmir when it was possible to travel there. He brought back spices and when he got back he said, "let's prepare a dinner" and it was really spicey!

MJ: We ate like Maharajahs!

J: He loved spicy flavors. He loved tasting everything.

MJ: He died in February, four years ago. He was fifty. He was really young. You just never think this kind of thing can happen.

J: We didn't close the bar. The bar is like a circus and the circus never stops and the bar never stops. We are always open even if one of us is ill. Somebody fills in.

His death, of course, had a huge effect on the bar, the kitchen... but the personal side was the most difficult. He had such a presence.

MJ: There was only one Albert.

TEMPORADA

JORDI

We have our regular dishes that we prepare every week. But the seasons bring new dishes, which we really like. We have summer dishes, *gazpachos*... In winter people like the *escudella*, and wild mushrooms in the fall. The customers like the fact that we change the menu to take advantage of the seasons.

MARÍA JOSÉ

And we'll say, "it's been a long time since we have done a rice dish, let's do an *arroz caldoso*." Or we'll see what's in season and mention it. And then we make it. There is always something good to cook.

JORDI

I keep everything in my head. but I have a Mac at home and once in a while I try to write something down but it's hard to sit down and do this after a day at Pinotxo. The first thing I do when I get home is settle the accounts, then I check emails, and after that it's really hard to do anything else. But it's easy to remember and you're prompted by things like what's next up seasonally.

I love seasonal food. When things are in season I cook it. When it is time for artichokes, we cook artichokes. Some people have artichokes all year long, but we don't. We have *Pimentos del Padrón* when it is their season, in summer. Now they are out of season but they are everywhere. We don't have *Pimentos del Padrón* now.

We take a lot of care selecting the ingredients. And with our kind of cooking, it's all about the ingredients. The customers can tell.

A TALE OF
TWO TEAMS

You might not know that there's another *La Liga* (the highest division of the Spanish football league) team from our fair city. Reial Club Deportiu Espanyol de Barcelona (or just Espanyol), founded in 1900 is just a year younger than FC Barcelona.

Calling themselves "Pericos" (parakeets) Espanyol fans consider the team to be a more real, pure, and genuine alternative to the flashy financial juggernaut called Barça which routinely pulls in over six hundred million euros a year. Jordi's support for the "other" team perhaps reflects why there isn't Patatas Bravas or Sangria on the menu. Can you say, "autentico?"

THE SHOW MUST GO ON

J: You have to keep moving forward. You have to continue. My brother was the manager and I was always there. We cooked different dishes. He was in control of the kitchen but it was more complicated than that.

We are a team and the Pinotxo team works really well together.

MJ: The big thing is you are so exposed there. Things get hot. Everything is always "live." Sometimes it's part of the show. Like Jordi says, the bar is a show and you always have to be on. Luckily, we are all pretty thin so we can move easily and quickly behind the bar. We rarely have problems.

Normally everything runs smoothly. But we are all human and have different moods. But the bar really is an enjoyable place.

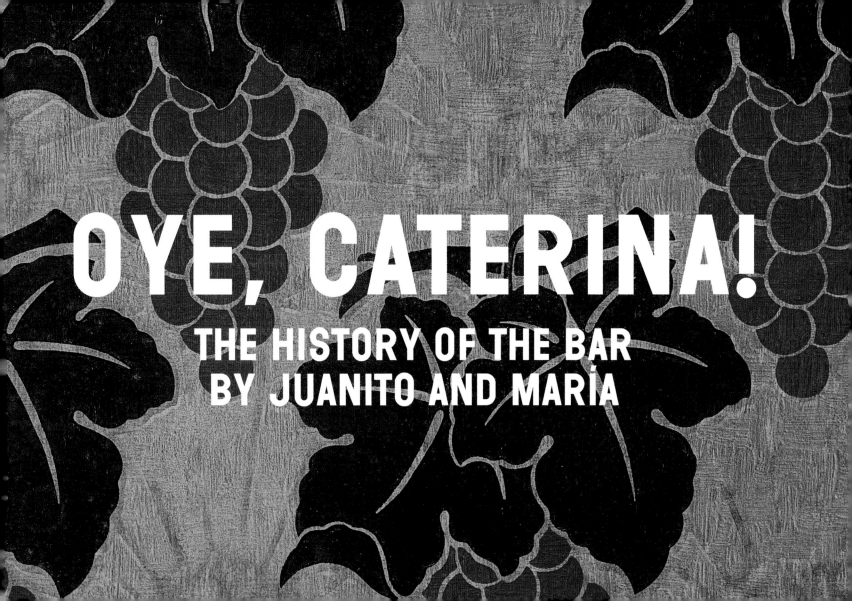

OYE, CATERINA!

THE HISTORY OF THE BAR
BY JUANITO AND MARÍA

CATERINA

MARÍA: My mother, Caterina, walked to Barcelona with my Grandfather from Andalusia.

JUANITO: Walking and nearly begging.

MARÍA: She was sixteen or seventeen and she went to the Boqueria to sell garlic, lemons, onions, nails...

She sold these kind of things standing outside of the Boqueria. That's how she made a living. She hadn't met my father yet.

It was in the early twenties, during the time of Alfonso XIII. I was born on April 27th, 1931 and Spain was declared a republic on the 7th of April, so I am a republican.

JUANITO: In the old days, in front of the markets, there were people selling things. They did this to survive because life was very hard. This is what our mother did.

M: She was living on Calle Mediodia.

J: That was in the heart of what was then called the Barrio Chino. It was a rough neighborhood with hard people but they didn't have any alternative. She didn't have any money to live anyplace else. She was with her father, and afterwards relatives from Andalusia started to arrive. My mother spent many years here with her father. Just the two of them. Then she met my father a few years later. They got married.

The Boqueria had a manager who saw that my mother was very honest and hardworking.

THERE HAS BEEN A MARKET AT OR NEAR
THE CURRENT LOCATION OF "EL MERCAT
DE SANT JOSEP DE LA BOQUERIA"
AKA "THE BOQUERIA" SINCE THE 13TH
CENTURY. THE BOQUERIA NOW HAS UP
TO 70 MILLION VISITORS ANNUALLY.
MY ADVICE, GO EARLY.

IT WASN'T FIREWORKS

MARÍA: I was eight years old when the *guerra civil* started.

JUANITO: I remember the bombings. There was a bomb shelter at the end of the street.

M: We were both born on Calle Aurora in the Barrio Chino... the Raval. Then we moved to Poble Sec.

J: ...Calle Murillo. I remember hearing the sirens which meant that the planes were coming. My father would take us outside to the balcony because we were scared. He said, "Hey look it's just fireworks." It wasn't fireworks.

M: Juanito couldn't breath because of asthma.

J: Then we would go down to the shelter. I vividly remember that there was a really strong smell of mildew and dampness.

M: After the war we suffered more from hunger than during the war. The franquistas would come by with a truck loaded with milk and chocolate and if we said, "*Viva Franco, arriba España*" they would give us a bit of bread and chocolate or a tin of milk.

J: That's the way the war was. Only the opportunists came out.

FRANCISCO FRANCO WAS FOND OF OFFERING UP HIS PEOPLE AS PRACTICE TARGETS FOR FELLOW FACISTS ITCHING TO TRY OUT THEIR NEW SHINY WAR MACHINES.
ON APRIL 26TH, 1936 HITLER AND THE LUFTWAFFE'S CONDOR DIVISION (WITH ITALIAN SUPPORT) GOT TO TRY OUT THEIR BRAND NEW TECHNIQUE CALLED "CARPET BOMBING" ON THE 7,000 INHABITANTS OF THE BASQUE VILLAGE OF GUERNICA.
ON MARCH 16TH, 1938 BENITO MUSSOLINI GOT BARCELONA ALL TO HIMSELF. THE ITALIAN AIR FORCE BOMBED BARCELONA AND ITS CITIZENS EVERY THREE HOURS FOR THREE CONSECUTIVE DAYS AND NIGHTS.

M: He liked her a lot. Everybody loved her.

J: This manager said to her, "Listen, Caterina, there's a bar for sale in the market. Why don't you buy it? If you don't have money I will lend it to you and you can buy it." That's how my mother got the bar.

M: No, it wasn't like that. She got help to buy the bar but because they didn't have any money, our father's boss, who had a construction business, invested in it and in exchange kept half the bar.

J: They set up a business, the two of them. My father's boss and my mother. Eventually my father's boss said, I don't want anything to do with the bar. I'm taking my cut and you can stay if you want. And that's when my mother really started running the bar.

Of all of the markets, I think we were the first in Barcelona to serve hot food.

You see, in the old days the bars in the markets only sold sandwiches, coffee, and pastries and that was it.

M: My father made a small inexpensive kitchen for my mother in the bar. It was just a counter.

J: So, because the other vendors in the Boqueria were so fond of my mother, someone like a butcher would say, "Oye Caterina, could you put this piece of meat in your soup? And when it's done I will come and get it." A woman who sold chickens would come in and say, "Caterina would you put this chicken thigh in your caldo? And when it's done I will come and get it."

And that's why this soup, which is typically Catalan, is called *Escudella i Carn d'olla*. Soup and meat from the same pot. So she'd sell the soup part and the other folks would retrieve what they had put in. The clients of the Boqueria used to say, "What a lovely soup they make here!" But it was because of all of the raw ingredients that she threw in, which were actually just on loan! And that's how my mother started to get known for her cooking.

M: And then there were *patatas fritas*. A butcher would bring in a steak and say, "Look, why don't you cook me this steak and then make me some *patatas fritas* to go with it?"

J: So my mother would charge to cook the steak and make the fries and the business started growing.

M: We were the only ones with hot food. I started working at the bar when I was nine.

J: Maria started working there with my mother. It was just the two of them. I joined them later and it was my mother, my sister, me, and a helper. Then the helper left and it was the three of us, then my mother left and it was just us two.

M: I was there for seventy years. I enjoyed cooking.

J: I was, shall we say, the public relations guy. When my mother was there, the cooking was basic but good. It was things that were typical of the time. *Caldos*, *Estofados*. But it was my sister who really gave the place a name and opened it up with a wider variety of dishes.

M: We changed the menu. We stopped offering *patatas fritas* as a side when someone brought us in a steak to cook for them. Instead we offered our own steak and *patatas fritas*.

LEFT TO RIGHT: JUANITO, CATERINA, JOSEP JR., JOSEP AND MARIA

FOOD

MARÍA
A lot of people have a different picture of the bar in their heads.

JUANITO
We're a very small place. They see it and they say, "We expected something different." But when they sit down and eat, they say, "Well, that was really worth it."

MARÍA
Fish-wise, Jordi sees what is available...

JUANITO
And then he decides what we'll do. We have many recipes and we change them most everyday.
The regular items; *rabo de buey*, the *calamarsets with fesols de Santa Pau*, the *garbanzos* with *morcilla*, the *cap-i-pota*. These have to be made everyday.

JUANITO
Cap-i-pota uses the snout of the pig, the morro. They called it *cap-i-pota* because in the old days they used the snout and a lamb shank.

MARÍA
No, it was veal.

JUANITO
OK, veal.

MARÍA
With *cap-i-pota* they used to put in the veal shank... *cap* head... *morro, pota* foot... veal shank.

JUANITO
Another important dish is *Calamarsets amb fesols de Santa Pau*.

MARÍA
Sauteed squid with small white beans from the village of Santa Pau. They turn out delicious.

JUANITO
And *Garbanzos* with *Morcilla* is really, really good as well.

MARIA
It was Albert who started doing these dishes.

JUANITO
We have the other things we don't make ourselves like the pastries; *ensaimadas* and croissants. Like the *Chuchos*. The guy that makes them says, "We only make them for you."

MARÍA
So when the guy who makes the *chuchos* dies...

JUANITO
No more *chuchos*!

MARÍA
With the *Ensaimadas* and croissants, if by lunchtime they haven't all been sold, we offer them for dessert.

JUANITO
We put the *ensaimadas* and croissants on the grill with a lot of sugar and we rub them around and they get caramelized; it's absolutely delicious.

MARÍA
We invented this.

JUANITO
I'll tell you something, when I go to a restaurant or a bar, wherever I go, I always check out what others do. Once I was in Zaragoza and I went into a bar to have a *café con leche*. I saw that they made it the way we now make *cortados* at the bar, with the multiple layers and the foam on top. I watched them and I thought I could do this in my bar. People would like it and it has been really popular.

PINOTXO 2.0

ALBERT AND FERRAN ADRIÀ DISCUSS GARBANZOS

M: My mother stopped working at sixty or so because she was frail from all the hard work.

When she stopped working, I took over the kitchen because I really enjoyed reading cookbooks and cooking and I liked doing more things. *Cap-i-pota*, *Callos*, it was a bit more sophisticated.

J: We developed a different working system. We bought the shrimp directly from the pescadors and cooked them right there on the spot. Instead of the customers bringing their own ingredients for us to cook, we bought the raw ingredients and got started little by little in this way.

M: So it was the two of us; and in the seventies and eighties my children started working at the bar.

J: First Albert and then Jordi.

M: Albert was very good in the kitchen.

J: Yes, Albert was great in the kitchen but Jordi is now also very good. From time to time the likes of Ferran Adrià and Juan María Arzak would drop by and say, "What a beautiful dish you've cooked for us today!"

M: We used to open at 4 a.m. and night people, those that were finishing work or whatever; they came to the bar and found...

J: ...whatever food they wanted. People like journalists who were working all night.

1. ALBERT
2. JUANITO
3. JOSEP
4. MAGDALENA
5. MARIA
6. CATERINA

CLOCKWISE FROM TOP LEFT: JUANITO AND CATERINA, JUANITO AND HIS OLDER BROTHER JOSEP, JUANITO AFTER CARRYING THE TORCH FOR THE 1992 OLYMPICS

M: We were allowed to open at whatever time we wanted. There wasn't a set time.

J: I was the one opening back then. Early in the morning I had people coming from everywhere. Show business people, even lots of prostitutes. People who spent the night on Las Ramblas... and before going to bed, they would come to the bar and eat their meat or stew or whatever, and then go off to sleep.

M: It was a world visited by another world.

J: Show business people were one thing, and the market people were a very different thing, and those from the barrio chino another thing again.

M: We even opened on Sunday mornings.

J: We never went on holidays. We got to a point when my sister and I were so exhausted that one year we thought we should try closing for a week in August and see what kind of response we would get. We thought that if the customers didn't come back after just a week, we'd just sell the bar. So we took a risk and took that week off, worrying about what would happen when we got back. When we got back everything was just the same. The same amount of customers, it was like we had never closed.

M: So the next year we added another week to our vacation.

J: So every year thereafter we took another week until we got to a month. Now we take off all of August.

RUNNING AND THE OLYMPICS

JUANITO
The bar's biggest popularity came with the Olympics in the nineties. It seemed like people knew Barcelona and the bar everywhere.

MARÍA
You had a lot to do with it. You are very open with everybody. Word of mouth works wonders.

JUANITO
Well, I've always been a very sociable person. A smile. A joke. A little something I say to a lady. Another little something I say to another lady. And I think this has made the bar well-known. When it's really busy and someone calls me Joan I don't always answer back. But if they call me Pinotxo, without fail, I answer back.

MARÍA
You are the Pinotxo of the bar. You always have a smile on your face.

JUANITO
Well, being attentive is really, really

important. And that there is a distance between me and the customer. There has to be mutual respect.

MARÍA

Running and working are Juanito's hobbies.

JUANITO

I never get tired. When I am finished at the bar I put on my tracksuit and go for a run. Usually for two or three hours. I did the first eighteen marathons in Barcelona and once the New York marathon.

MARÍA

In ninety-two you got to carry the torch for the Olympics.

JUANITO

I told some friends who were the organizers of the games, "Listen, I want to carry the Olympic Torch." And they said, "Yeah sure. Why would you carry the torch? There are so many people who want to do it." So I said, "Do whatever you have to do, but I want to do it." So a few days later I get this phone call, "Señor Juan?"

"Speaking." "We would like to inform you that you will be carrying the Olympic torch." So these friends came by and I told them, "Hey! I'm carrying the torch!" And they said, "Listen, we know, don't talk to us anymore about the torch, we've had it up to here." And I said, "OK, OK, I just want to ask one more thing. Wouldn't it be nice if I could carry the torch on the Las Ramblas leg, you know in front of the Boqueria?" And they said, "Juan, don't push it." So a few days later I get another phone call. "Señor Juan?" "Speaking." "Yes, listen, we would like to inform you that your section of the run will be Las Ramblas." So in the end they did everything for me. I ran past the market and everybody came out to applaud. It was something else!

AWARD NIGHT

IT takes a long time for a project to go from inspiration to something you can hold, smell, touch and in this case, hopefully sell. It requires stamina, conviction ,and in the case of my collaborators, a huge amount of understanding and patience. There are some benefits to long term projects. This book for example, has allowed me to eat well and regularly and to, on occasion steal things from the plates of complete strangers. Having said that, the phrase "**WEAR OUT YOUR WELCOME**" comes to mind as I've seen incredibly warm, heartfelt greetings and regular offers of free *chuchos* turn to eye rolls and questions of "**¿QUÉ PASA?**" and "**OYE TÍO, ¿CUÁNDO?**" But if it takes a village to raise a child it takes an apparently really long time to finish a book like this.

One of the events that transpired during my extended stay at Pinotxo was that Juanito was awarded the "**PREMI DE GASTRONOMIA**" by the city of Barcelona. Considering that our town and the region are not exactly shy of culinary rock stars, like the brothers **ADRIÀ** and **ROCA**, **CARLES GAIG**, **CARLES ABELLAN**, **FERMÍ PUIG**, our friend **CARME RUSCADELLA** (to name but a few), and countless astounding but less well

known cocineros, this was a very big deal. As Juanito and the gang are inherently shy and honestly humble, I was informed about this from someone outside of the **PINOTXO UNIVERSE**. Soon the papers were all over the story. The aforementioned culinary elite were falling all over themselves to offer their praises, and I was in scramble mode. Sadly another damnable inspiration materialized. I've got it! Let's make a film! I imposed my vision on yet another collaborator, my friend and freelance cameraman Alfonso Beato, who I pulled away from his knee surgery recovery to document the big event. We grabbed his and a second camera and hit the bar. True to form, it was just another day for the equipo but Juanito did allow himself to leave an hour early to swap out his vest and bow tie for a fashionable tux.

Attempting the documentarians prime directive of not interfering with alien civilizations, Alfonso and I followed Juanito home and tried to fade into the woodwork as he spruced himself up for the ceremony, which was to be held at the **SALÓ DE CENT**, Catalunya's historic and most hallowed hall of governance. We covered him shaving, dressing, and putting on his shoes and socks. We did, however, draw the line at getting in the shower with him.

All three of us hopped in a cab (well, considering his knee, for Alfonso it was more or less an awkward crawl) and headed off. From the back seat we listened in as the celebrated and much loved restaurateur compared notes with the portly cab driver about where to get the best bowl of barnacles (*percebres*) and which country had the most beautiful women.

We arrived at Barcelona's famous Plaça Sant Jaume ,and soon after Juanito disappeared into the gothic bowels of the beating heart of the **AJUNTAMENT** (as Barcelona's city government is called). We next caught up with the maestro as he received his award from Ada Colau, our fair city's radical and cool *alcadessa* (mayor) and repeatedly arrested former activist. Grasping the award, a big, thick and very proletarian plywood "B", he told a room full of dignitaries and all of Catalunya via TV3 (the Catalan television network) just how humbled and honored he was by the city's acknowledgment of all those decades making triple decker cortados and conversation with regular folks, international celebrities, night owl journalists, the occasional lady of the evening, and hungry customers from all over the world.

For me it was an honor to have been able to witness such an event, and, for Alfonso, I suspect it was well worth the permanent limp he seems to have acquired.

María

One of the great rewards of this project has been getting to know the Bayén Asín family. It's one thing to sit at the bar and exchange quick chit chat with Juanito (because, let's face it, the man's really busy) and quite another to be invited to the apartment that he shares with his sister and Jordi's mother María.

We invaded their home for a few hours and learned much about the bar's origins. We heard stories from both the good times and the bad, about Juanito's passion for running and *las mujeres*, and how María's love of cooking translated into decades tending the stove at Pinotxo. It was a very special and privileged evening.

Spain is a place where life is up front and personal twenty-four hours a day, seven days a week. The guy from the *estanco* (tobacco shop) sees you at the *panadería* and asks about your family. The woman from the *panadería* sees you at the *estanco* and asks if your cold is better. The frail old lady who sits on the bench in front of the waxing parlor asks about how you are handling the weather, six times a day. People's lives are woven tightly together. You start to wonder about things like if the occasionally grumpy lady who is sometimes at the *estanco* is the guy's sister or wife, and couldn't the owner of the bakery hire a helper for your friend so she wouldn't have to bake at least eight kinds of bread, four kinds of croissant, and three kinds of "muffis" (muffins... formerly known as *madalenas*), bag up all the commercial orders, and still give you five cents back in change for your sixty-five cent baguette. And when "Carmen", the frail old lady, is not on the bench asking you about the weather, you find yourself worrying about her.

I checked in with Jordi after *las vacaciones*, (Pinotxo like many of the small businesses in Spain, closes for the month of August). In my *"castellano de monos"* I asked about their break and Jordi responded that it went well except that his mother had died.

What do you say? What can you say? Although I had just met her, I thought about her and how she and Juanito would complete each other's sentences, and how fond their two very overweight, slightly fragrant dogs were of adhering themselves to my leg in hopes of even more contact. I thought of drinking a beer with Juanito in their kitchen. Although eighty one, he had just got back from a three hour run and was dressed in a hoody, flashy track pants, and well worn, real deal Nikes. I thought about María telling me that when she began cooking, she poured over cookbooks looking for special recipes. She wanted the food at the bar to be more elegant, "you know, I wanted to cook things like *callos*."

THE PEOPLE

JUANITO

Truly, this bar has a lot of history. My mother started working in this bar. Then, after my mother it was my sister. After my sister it was me, and now, the children of my sister. It has been four generations who went through here and I hope it continues.

It was a bar like the rest here in the Boqueria. And we, little by little, introduced several other things. We started doing meals, and we became a small restaurant. And it is a small restaurant still, and here we are.

I think there are several reasons why we are famous. First is the quality of the ingredients we provide. Second, the character of those who work with us. These guys are great; they are awesome. They are very friendly with people. Kindness is a big issue.

We work here six days a week... Monday to Saturday. Now we open at six o'clock in the morning. But, many years ago we opened at four. Then workers came from all the nightclubs and cabarets in Barcelona. When they closed, they came here to eat before they went to sleep. And here we began to gain a bit of notoriety. Radio broadcasters came and made programs here. People came saying, "**HEY, JUANITO. YESTERDAY...**" I heard you on the radio.

I ran the first eighteen marathons in Barcelona. And I've run a marathon in New York. I was born an athlete. I do not smoke, I do not drink. My only fault is that I like the ladies. I think that everyone is born the way they are. I do not know if sport has given me this life or what, but this year I turn eighty-one. I mean, I've reached the top.

This is also another story of mine. There was an owner of a great restaurant. His name was Ramon Cabau. He was a very famous man. He came every day for lunch here. Every day. One day he comes and tells me: "**HEY, JUANITO. I'M SICK OF SEEING YOU WITHOUT A BOW TIE.**" He always wore bow ties. He said, "**TAKE THIS ONE. I WANT YOU TO WEAR IT... FOREVER.**" And since then I have worn a bow tie.

When the time comes, I will retire. I am a person who thanks God, and I do not expect anything from anyone. However, the day I take a glass and my hand trembles; it will be the time to retire. However, meanwhile, this is my life.

There have been many celebrities who have come here. Like the journalist Carlos Herrera... Woody Allen. A friend of mine came here with a beautiful woman and said: "**JUANITO, I PRESENT ...**" I was busy, and I said, "**HI, HOW ARE YOU? BON DIA.**" And he said: "**JUANITO, DON'T YOU KNOW WHO THIS IS?**" And when I saw her, I apologized. It was Jacqueline Bisset. She was super, super... Super!

I don't eat much here, because we work all the time. I have my coffee with milk. Then I eat a bit at noon. Because here you cannot eat as you want because the customer needs you. And customers are first and nothing else.

When I leave work at five in the afternoon. I go home; I put on my running shoes, and then I go run to clear my mind. I go there. I go with my thoughts... I run for a couple of hours around Montjuïc.

JORDI

I am the third-generation. My grandmother started the bar. After that, my mother, my grandmother, and my uncle worked together. Then there was my mother and my uncle. Then, my uncle, my brother, and I. Now it's my uncle and I. It is a bar that has been open for many years. It is an obligatory place to go in Barcelona.

When I was young, I came to help out my family after school. I came to help on Saturdays too. It's something you have inside.

Before the Olympics, Barcelona was a city that was not well known worldwide. After the Olympics, it became a major tourist attraction, and many people came.

MARÍA JOSÉ

I became part of this family because of Jordi, who I had met in Tenerife where I am from. I am here basically for love. **THE KITCHEN IS RUN BY THE BOYS. THIS IS VERY RARE BECAUSE COOKING IS USUALLY DONE BY WOMEN.**

Working here is great because it is an open place where, besides our regular customers, you meet different people. We always have fun. But we work very hard. There are moments of stress because of the amount of people. You want to take care of everyone the best way possible, but sometimes you can't, and that causes stress. Other than that, everything is very pleasant.

The boys working here are my sons, not biologically, but they are my sons. I have known some of them since they were three years old, they have slept over in my house. They have studied with my children. People sometimes ask me if they are mine.

ALBERT

I have been working here for eight years.

Working here is great. Every day we work 10 hours, Monday through Saturday. I like to work here in the Boqueria.

My favorite dish is the *gambas a la plancha*. And the *rabo*.

I like everything I do here. If you have to scrub, you scrub. If you cook, you cook. If you have to serve, you serve. We all pitch in. The customers are all pleasant people, they are very polite, and they never are in a hurry.

I feel like I am part of the family. And at Christmas I go to Jordi and Maria Jose's house for dinner on Christmas Day and on San Esteban's Day. Everything is perfect, it's home.

DÍDAC

My name is Dídac. I'm 26 years old. I'm Jordi and María José son.

My sister and I spent a lot of our childhood here at the bar. I used to run around and play at the Boqueria. When I was a teenager I came to lend a hand when I was not at school, and on the weekends, and on school holidays, summers. Now I'm working here full time.

I'm learning everything here by watching, listening, and doing. I'm slowly taking it all in.

DANIEL

My name is Daniel. I am from the Philippines. I am 33 years old. I wash dishes and do prep work. I started here in 2013. I start in the morning at 8 and I work until noon. My favorite dish to prep is the *rabo*. It's a great dish.

JAVI

My name is Javi. I am a sex machine.

I have been working for 7 years at Pinotxo.

I am the go boy. I go here. I go there. I cook. I do everything.

I started washing dishes and then other kitchen work; you wash the dishes, then you cook, and then to the customers.

I think Jordi is the best boss you can have in the world. For me he is not a boss but a friend. I talk to him about everything. He never gets angry. Juanito's great too. We laugh a lot. María Jose is like another Mom to me. I can't complain about my bosses. On the other hand, I can and do complain about my colleagues.

Juanito is a man with a special devotion for his work. He loves his job. But awhile ago we changed the espresso machine. Juanito wasn't crazy about that.

My favorite dish is the chiperones with the fesols. But basically, I like everything,

People who come here aren't customers, they're friends. OK some of the girls come here as customers but they leave as girlfriends.

OLIVIA

I'm Olivia, I'm the daughter of Jordi and María José.

My favorite dish here is the *rabo* which is the best in Barcelona. It's super good.

I grew up at the bar. I came here every day to see my parents. My parents wanted to spend as much time with us as possible.

It was fun to come here when I was little. I played at the Boqueria and I served food too.

ESTHER

I'm Esther and I work from one thirty until we close, six days a week. I prep and wash dishes. I've been here for eight years.

WHERE TO FIND ALL THIS STUFF?

It's a lot easier to find "Spanish stuff" now than it was after my first trip to Spain decades ago. On trips back to the USA I used to bring back rustic-looking bags of fabada beans and *arroz bomba*, cute cans of *Pimentón de La Vera*, Ortiz tuna, and the occasional stuffed "**CALAMARES EN SU TINTA**" (squid in its own ink) or "**OREJAS GUISADAS CON JAMÓN**" (pigs ears stewed with jamon), just to freak out my less gastronomically adventurous friends and family. But now things like high quality *bonito del norte* and *Pimentón* can be found at Whole Pay Check and other swanky supers (OK, stewed *orejas* might take a little bit longer to be adopted). Still, there's a lot of really basic stuff that is still hard to come by. Those short little noodles called "**FIDEOS**" for example. Yes, you can find something called "**FIDEOS**" in latino markets and in big box stores like Winco that cater to that market. Although both kinds are short noodles and look more or less the same, latino *fideos* and Spanish *fideos* are really something different. No disrespect, but I've tried to make a **FIDEUÀ** with the latino variety and it just goes all gooey. And Mario Batalla, you may think you can make a *fideuà* with busted up fedellini, shrimp, bacon, cilantro, lime juice, cinnamon, ginger, and tofurkey (OK, I lied about the tofurkey) but there will be a night when you'll be visited by the ghost of Guifré el Pilós (See "Sofregit", page 78) who will in no uncertain terms show you the difference between a number 2 and a number 4 fideo. Truthfully, his dish doesn't sound half bad but folks, it's not a *fideuà*. Can we have a little respect for all the *abuelas* who for centuries have been discussing noodle diameter and whether the liquid to pasta ratio should be 1.5 to 1 or 1.75 to 1? *Collons*! Ginger!!!

Chipirones (squid babies) are another difficult item. Again you might think you can go to the fish counter at Ralph's, buy those lily white ultra sterilized prophylactic stand-ins they call "calamaris", chop them up and call it done. In fact, it's not done and it's not right. *Chipirones* are tiny little guys who come *entero*... whole, with their little footies and noggins (but *sans* quills and beaks). In the case of Pinotxo's famous **CALAMARSETS AMB FESOLS DE SANTA PAU,** they are really integral to the delicate dance of flavors of *el mar* (the sea) and the mountains (*montanya*).

Even *bacalao*, which has been designed to be "carry on" since somebody figured out that you could lash a couple of logs together and get the hell out of wherever, is not all that easy to locate. When it comes to salt cod, my adage has always been, "when in doubt ask an Italian."

Truth be told, in the Estados Unidos you have but two reliable national sources of "typically Spanish" *productos*:

LA TIENDA
WWW.LATIENDA.COM
This is a family operation that, in the sixties, began their love affair with all things Spanish, when patriarch and Navy Chaplain, Don Harris, was stationed near Cadiz. These folks have been nurturing *el duende* for a very long time, and have been a good source for *"cosas muy autentico"* in North America for over twenty years. In addition to food items, they also are a decent source for Spanish cookware. They have a retail shop in Williamsburg, Virginia.

CONVERSA
WWW.CONSERVASHOP.COM
In 2004 Leslie and Manuel Recio created Viridian Farms in Oregon's fertile Willamete Valley, and introduced such exotic crops as *Calçots* and *Pimentos del Padrón*. Thier new venture Conserva, features the best of the best canned, jarred and preserved products from Spain, France and Portugal. Think of Conserva as your personal online *Colmado* (a small neighborhood grocery store featuring high quality, traditional products).

THE SPANISH TABLE
WWW.SPANISHTABLE.COM
Like La Tienda, The Spanish Table began with a trip to Cadiz. Hmmm... Perhaps a trip down south is in order. Also like La Tienda, this family operation has been sneaking in illegal hams for a couple of decades. Ask for Paco. Just kidding... In addition to being online, they have a number of real brick and mortar stores on the west coast of the USA.

1 800 CHIPIRONES
WWW.BARPINOTXOTHEBOOK.COM
Undoubtedly, suppliers of the real, real deal will only become more prevalent in the future. Please keep an eye on our website for breaking news regarding sources for infant celapods and odd ball cuts of meat.

RECIPES

SAMFAINA

Perhaps the most fundamental dish of all is *samfaina*. It's a sauce. It's a side. It's a dessert topping. Let this be known: For all intents and purposes *samfaina* is... Ratatouille. The Catalans say they introduced it to the south of France when they were in control of the Cote d'Azur. OK, so be it. But it also is, more or less, identical to Pisto (not to be confused with "**PESTO**") which comes from La Mancha. And then there is Bashed Neeps (mashed turnips) from Scotland which has nothing to do with *samfaina* but it's a great name. Call it what you will, this dish works well as a side, under a piece of *bacallà*, a fried egg, or a chicken thigh. Or as a topper on rice or couscous. Or simply as a sauce for your thick, saucy needs. Pinotxo's version is special because of the addition of raisins, pine nuts, and a little semi-sweet white wine. And to this I say, "**WHY NOT?**"

Serves many... just add more ingredients to scale.

4	medium onions, thinly sliced
1	eggplant, cubed
1	large zucchini, quartered lengthwise and then cut into 5 cm (2 in) pieces
2	nyora peppers (See "Provisions", page 67). Soak them for at least two hours and then scrape out the pulp. Discard the skins.
2	green "Italian" peppers, seeded, halfed lenghtwise and cut into 5 cm (2 in) pieces (See "The Problem with Peppers", page 131)
1	red bell pepper, seeded, quartered and cut into 5 cm (2 in) pieces
6	smallish, ripe tomatoes, peeled, seeded, and grated (See "*El secret del tomàquet beneït*", page 76)
	raisins, a palm full
	pine nuts, a smaller palm full
175 ml	(6 oz) semi-sweet white wine (You could also use *moscatel* or saki... no, not saki.)
	extra virgin olive oil
	salt

1. Toast the pine nuts lightly in a little olive oil and reserve. Don't burn them! They brown fast.
2. Cover the bottom of a pot or cazuela with a hearty pour of olive oil and bring up to medium temperature.
3. Add the onions, lower the heat and "*sofregir*" (See "*Sofregit*", page 78) the onions until they are translucent and golden.
4. Add the peppers, nyora pulp, raisins, eggplant, and stirring when required, cook until soft.
5. Add the grated tomatoes, wine, the zucchini and again, cook until soft.
6. Add the previously toasted pine nuts and salt to taste.

PA AMB TOMÀQUET

FÀCIL!

pa de pagès or ciabatta (here, there
is much discussion about which
is correct, but either is equally
delicious)

extra virgin olive oil

a few cloves of unpeeled garlic

flakey sea salt

tomàquets

1 Take a slice of decent and "airy" pa de pagès
(a round country loaf... not a baguette) or a
ciabatta sliced in half, and toast it. OK, over on
the right I know I said the bread should be stale,
and one could imagine that this is the origin of
the form, but most everybody I know just uses
the toaster and saves the stale bread for bread
crumbs.
2 Take an unpeeled clove of garlic and slice it in half.
Take one of the halves and rub the cut side all over
the bread.
3 Cut a ripe "smallish" tomato in half laterally
(again, originally, tomatoes were used that were
well past their prime but these days just make
sure they are really, really ripe). Whilst squeezing
the tomàquet, rub the bread with it. If you are
channeling your inner Jordi or Montse, you will
be able to use one tomato half to coat at least
two pieces of bread.
4 Dribble or drown the operation with the olive oil.
5 Sprinkle on some quality salt.
6 If you are dainty, cut the bread in two and eat. If
not, just eat it.

**IF THERE IS ONE DISH THAT REALLY REPRESENTS THE BEAT-
ING HEART OF CATALAN CUISINE IT'S PAN CON TOMATE, OR
MORE APPROPRIATELY, EN CATALÀ "PA AMB TOMÀQUET." PA
AMB TOMÀQUET REPRESENTS THREE MAIN CATALAN VIR-
TUES; FRUGALITY, COMMON SENSE AND TO "APROFITAR,"
WHICH MEANS "TO MAKE THE BEST OF THINGS" OR, DEPEND-
ING ON WHO YOU ARE TALKING TO, "TO GET SOMETHING FOR
NOTHING." LET'S BE HONEST, ALTHOUGH THE CATALANS ARE
SOME OF THE MOST EMOTIONALLY GENEROUS PEOPLE ON
THE PLANET, THEY HAVE A REPUTATION OF BEING A LITTLE
STINGY.** This is probably an unfair appraisal but you will never
confuse them for Andalusians whose bar owners aggressively com-
pete for which establishment can hand out the most free food to
accompany a one buck beer or who will get in a fist fight over who is
picking up the tab. In Catalunya profunda, if you want a plate of almonds or two or three olives, by God, you are going to pay for them.

Having said that, a very tasty of dishes can be made from ingredients way past their sell by date, namely stale bread and overly ripe
tomatoes.

This is eaten for breakfast, for a snack, at lunch, dinner, and probably clandestinely at four a.m. during a pee-pee break.

You may if, you wish, add some trozos finos de jamon Ibérico or
anchovies or some escalivada and boom... lunch is served.

Please note, if you deviate from the order presented here, two
things will happen: 1. The Ghost of Guifré el Pilós (See "**SOFRE-
GIT**", page 78) will visit you and curse your botifarra (a fat and juicy
Catalan sausage) and 2. you will wind up with soggy and un-garlicy
pa amb tomaquet.

Techniques
AND
Trucos

EL SECRET DEL TOMÀQUET BENEÏT

Are Catalans brilliantly thrifty or thrifty with their brilliance? Let's go with the former because these folks are just plain smart.

For example, the Catalans claim that they invented both the submarine and the helicopter. While this very well may be true, in my humble opinion, their most valuable contribution to mankind is how people form a simple queue. Granted, when a line of people gets cumbersome, they will resort to using one of those take-a-number-gadgets, but for *colas* (lines) under, say twelve people, they automatically implement this absolutely brilliant technique for maintaining order and reducing stress.

It's simple. When you arrive at a *parada* (stand), or a bank, or a *ferreteria* (which is a hardware store and not, as you might have guessed, a shop that specializes in selling ferrets), you just ask out loud, "who's last?" Not "who's next", but "who's last". "*Qui és l'últim?*" The last person in line says, "*Sóc jo!*" Which does not mean "suck" or "suck it up home boy, get in line!" It means "I am!" In acknowledgement you give a little head nod to that person. Here's the magic of this "truco". As long as you are more or less within their line of sight, you can go get a cup of coffee, buy some stuffed peppers, or have a chat with your buddy who sells artichokes from out by the airport (and no, it's an urban myth, jets do not dump excess AV fuel on them as they make their final approach). You just casually keep an eye on your contact (as they are theirs). No anxiety, no strange little power trips, no open carry weapons drawn, no moving along in an uncomfortable, over orderly fashion. No invasions of personal space. No eye contact issues. Like I said, it's brilliant, and by itself might, just be reason enough to move here.

But rest assured, Catalan Grandma genius extends well beyond social behavior experiments; they have perfected a technique for skinning and pulping tomatoes. And as most of the recipes in this book call for tomatoes specifically prepared in this manner, you would do well to pay special attention to this next part.

EL SECRETO

CUT YOUR TOMATOES IN HALF LATERALLY.

Squeeze the seeds out of the cut tomato. Slap the de-seeded tomato down onto one of those old school flat, square or triangular cheese graters which is hovering over a bowl. Then, with an open palm, rub the tomato back and forth on the coarse grating surface... being careful not to allow hand or tomato skin to pass through the grater. If all goes well, you should wind up with an intact palm holding a spent tomato skin and a bowl containing seedless, skinless tomato pulp goodness). *Molt bé.*

BÁSICOS

SOFREGIT

YOUR CATALAN VERB FOR TODAY IS "SOFREGIR", WHICH MEANS TO FRY LIGHTLY, ALTHOUGH I SUSPECT SLOWLY IS PROBABLY A MORE APPROPRIATE ADVERB. A SOFREGIT (SOFRITO IN CASTELLANO) IS A SLOW-COOKED MIXTURE OF VEGETABLES WITH AN EMPHASIS MOST OFTEN ON ONION AND TOMATOES, THAT IF MADE CORRECTLY, ENDS UP BEING A WONDERFULLY FLAVORFUL "JAMMY" CONCOCTION.

Unless it's for ice cream it seems like just about every Catalan recipe begins with "**FIRST MAKE A SOFREGIT**", so it's important that you know how to make the real deal.

IT'S ALSO A WAY OF CHANNELING YOUR INNER GUIFRÉ EL PILÓS (WILFRED THE HAIRY), AN 8TH CENTURY COUNT OF BARCELONA AND THE FATHER OF CATALAN NATIONALISM, WHO, WOUNDED DURING A BATTLE WITH EITHER THE MOORS OR THE NORMANS, DRUG HIS BLOODY FINGERS DOWN THE FRONT OF HIS SHIELD, THUS CREATING THE "SENYERA" (THE CATALAN COAT OF ARMS AND FLAG). WHAT'S A LITTLE BIT OF STIRRING COMPARED TO DRAGGING YOUR BATTLE-BLOODIED HAND DOWN YOUR SHIELD TO MAKE A POLITICAL POINT? STIR SLOWLY AND METHODICALLY. MAKE THE HAIRY ONE PROUD.

AND THEN...

YOU WILL NEED...

3 or more onions, sliced coarsely. In Catalunya, most cooks use an onion called *Figueres,* which one might (correctly) assume comes from somewhere near the town of Figueres, which is the former stomping grounds of Salvador Dali and home to his very strange but wonderful museum. Truth be told, just about any old yellow onion will do but sweeter onions like Walla Wallas are a little closer in flavor to the local variety.

3 ripe, medium-sized tomatoes, peeled, seeded, and grated (See *"El secret del tomàquet beneït"*, page 76)

1 In a *cazuela* or a large frying pan put a goodly portion of olive oil, maybe a centimeter or 1/8 of an inch (I know it seems like a lot but Spanish folks have one of the longest life expectancies in Europe, so just pour it in) and let it come up to temperature.

2 Add the onions and reduce the heat to a simmer. Stir occasionally. With time the onions should caramelize and become golden. Here's where you can test your patience. Some say that the onions of a good sofregit should be almost black but not burned. Hmmm... My patience usually lasts until the golden stage but if you have the right temperament go for it. Another indicator I have noticed is that the onion bits get progressively stickier as they cook... I suspect this is caused by the sugars being converted from the starches in the onions... or something like that. What you don't want is the sort of crispy, grilled onions that you would put on a hamburger. These are much, much softer and less distinct. Just go lower with the heat and slower than you are comfortable with. I usually time this by drinking a glass of red wine while I am cooking. When the wine is done... so are the onions. Just don't gulp.

3 Add the grated tomatoes and, continuing with the occasional stir... let them and the onions become one. Listen, I know I'm going to *get notes* on adding the tomatoes from the Policia Culinaria de Catalunya but there really are lots of recipes that have the addition of tomatoes. Try it both ways, I mean, how bad can onions and tomatoes be? Don't forget to add *una mica de sal*.

Adding finely minced garlic (just toss them in at the end of the onion phase) is also more or less legal. Adding chocolate chips and/or jalapeño peppers... is not. Please feel free to make a whack of *sofregit* with or without tomatoes and keep it a tupper in the refrigerator. Like leftover pizza, it's a wonderful thing to discover.

WHAT IS A PICADA?

A *picada* is another mysterious element from times when men wore tights, codpieces, and pointy shoes. What is it? When you remove a thousand years of stories and recipe futzing you wind up with basically a thickening agent like a roux in French and Cajun fare, or cornstarch in Cantonese cooking. Yes, ingredient or flavor-wise, it's much more complex than either of these forms, but the reason is the same: to thicken the texture and to round out the flavors. Unlike a roux or Chinese "**VELVETING**", the starches in a picada come from not just wheat or corn flour, but from a range of nuts, toasted bread, and occasionally *carquinyolis*, the Catalan equivalent of a biscotti.

Broken down further, there is a distinct **MOLE/PESTO VIBE** as well but I suspect these similarities are probably just happenstance. These ancient recipes come from times well before the introduction of wheat, corn, or even potatoes; when starches and vegetable proteins came from foraged things like chestnuts, *piñones* (pine nuts), walnuts, and hazelnuts. I suspect the origins of *picada* are as simple as this: someone wanted to thicken up a soup so they added the starches they had… and over a thousand years of adjusting and improvising, and the cultural influences of both invading and being invaded (as expressed by chocolate, cinnamon, parsley, garlic, and cumin), they wound up with this varied and fascinating adjunct. Most of my Catalan friends can't really explain exactly what this **MOLE/PESTO VIBE** tastes like, but they sure can tell when it's missing.

Here's Pinotxo's version. The addition of an anchovy really ups the dark and full flavor "**UMAMI**" quotient.

2 large garlic cloves, peeled and chopped finely

1 green "Italian" pepper, chopped finely (See "The Problem with Peppers", page 131)

a small bunch of parsley, chopped finely

1 anchovy

5 almonds, toasted and with skin removed, crushed

5 roasted hazelnuts, crushed

2 *carquinyolis* (these are exactly like hazelnut biscotti), broken into pieces

salt

---

1 Put a little salt in a mortar and add the garlic. Crush the garlic with the pestle and then gradually add the toasted almonds, hazelnuts, and the *carquinyolis*. Add the green pepper, anchovy, and a few parsley leaves. Continue to work the pestle. Add a few spoonfuls of the liquid from the dish to which you'll be adding the picada to. Continue mixing until you have made a thick paste. Then, when called for, add the picada to the dish and let it dissolve, then stir it in.

It's used in only one dish here (*Suquet de Rap*) and we'll let you know when to deploy.

DUENDE

"There is something in the dirt."

It was three o'clock in the morning and I was having a beer on the terrace of Mariola (from Granada) and Evert (from Holland) and trying to make sense of something. It was the noche de San Juan. July fifteenth. The equinox. The day that *Españoles* burn stuff like unloved couches and dining room tables and (occasionally) inadvertently light small children on fire. We were watching the store-bought fireworks that the neighbors were launching from their balconies and roofs into the interior courtyard, or *patio manzana*. *Patio manzanas* are the huge, empty centers of the blocks that, in the mid-eighteen hundreds, Ildefons Cerdà had designed in a massive architectural socio-economic fever dream to serve as a community-encouraging egalitarian park for the surrounding buildings. In the five-hundred and twenty nearly identical snub-cornered, hollow-centered blocks of Cerda's Eixample, only a few wound up serving this purpose. The majority of these vast spaces generally stood abandoned, or at best, were little-used (do you really need the equivalent of a soccer field in which to hang your laundry?) Occasionally they ended up poorly purposed as metal smelters, breweries, or later on as the roofs of ground floor supermarkets or car washes. Still, they allowed folks like Mariola and Evert (who inhabited the planta principal) to watch bottle rockets rain down on the neighbor's drying underwear, while dining *al fresco* during this region's many temperate months. And yes, to admire the few tomatoes growing from their terracotta planters.

I was struggling with my Castellano, as I continue to do to this day, to articulate exactly what I meant. *"En España existe una alma, una cosa, no se... anima, dentro de tierra... una cosa viejo, basico, primordial..."* Evert gave me a head nod but Mariola was still and silent. Maybe she was trying to figure out what my monkey Spanish meant, or maybe she was thinking about how poorly the tomatoes were doing, considering that Barcelona has on average over twenty-five hundred hours of sunshine per year, or maybe my *guiri* (a lobster red anglo-saxon) quasi new age spirituality was boring her. But I feel now as I felt then that there is something in the dirt here, something below the surface. Call it mauna, call it "grigri", call it voodoo or perhaps more appropriately call it *"duende."*

What's *"duende"*? There are two meanings. One describes sort of a leprechaun which inhabits the forests of northern Spain, and the other is an Andalusian term meaning to have "soul", or a profound sense of authenticity. This latter meaning is expressed in song, dance, performance, a piece of art or, if stretched a bit, a bowl of *estofado*. You can feel it when you see it, when you hear it, taste it, or smell it but it's really hard to describe in words. Federico García Lorca tried, "The duende, then, is a power, not a work. It is a struggle, not a thought... Meaning this: it is not a question of ability, but of true, living style, of blood, of the most ancient culture, of spontaneous creation." Heady stuff.

Chef and now famous restaurateur, John Gorham, came to Spain a decade ago, and felt this *intangible ánimo*. He has since built a wildly popular "Spanish" restaurant in my hometown of Portland, Oregon to explore exactly what this *"duende"* is. Granted, his recipes are often not exactly "traditional" but they may be all the more "authentic" because of it. And the constant block-long line in front of Gorham's *"Toro Bravo"* must mean something, no?

Maybe some of us *guiris* are just a little more sensitive to *"duende"* because we come from a place where our own sense of deep connectedness has been eroded by glowing screens, shiny gadgets, selfies, endless cults of celebrity, and where points of view are always skewed to the future rather to a living, breathing present that has been carved from the past. There really is something in the dirt. There is *"duende"* at Pinotxo. You can taste it.

BÁSICOS

txo bar

ALL I OLI

Listen up. This is your Catalan Grandma talking. If you are going to find your inner Jordi or Montserrat you need to learn how to make *all i oli*.

And just what is Ah-ye-ee-oh-lee? Some might say that it is "**GARLIC MAYON-NAISE**" and they would not be completely incorrect. Some might say that it is another one of those medieval miracles that can only be conjured if you live in a small *poble* of seventeen people, are at least a ninety-year old *l'avi* (Grandfather), are missing three fingers, and have been smoking three packs of filterless cigarettes a day since you were seven. Truth is, it's both, and both are worthy of your attention.

**WE GIVE YOU NOW TWO VERSIONS. LET'S START WITH THE L'AVI VERSION, WHICH WE SHALL CALL *ALL I OLI* "A POC A POC."
WHICH TRANSLATES BASICALLY TO: "DAD? ARE WE THERE YET?"
YOU WILL NEED A MORTAR AND PESTLE AND A SQUEEZY BOTTLE.**

ALL I OLI
"A POC A POC"
VERSION

6	cloves of garlic, peeled and minced
250 ml	(8 oz) extra virgin olive oil (loaded into a standard issue squeezy bottle)
1/4	of a cuchara (teaspoon) of salt (more or less, saltiness is pretty subjective)
1	squirt of lemon juice (optional)

Part 1:

1 Put the salt in a largish ceramic mortar (marble ones are pretty but they are porous). The classic Español ones are ceramic, yellow, and come with a wooden pestle. Get one.

2 Add the garlic and mash it into a paste with the pestle.

Part 2:

3 Now, sitting on a stool in a full upright position, clutch the mortar between your legs (yep... trust me) and using your dominant hand, and a rolling, machine-like circular motion (traditionalists say you should always churn in the same direction... however if you are in the southern hemisphere...), move the pestle 'round the mortar.
While this is going on, your other hand should be clutching the squeezy bottle and "a poc a poc", (which now means "little by little") dribbling in the olive oil, drop by drop. Incorporating the oil should take somewhere between 15 minutes and 3 and a half days. Seriously, figure around 20 to 30 minutes to emulsification.
Once the stuff is looking pretty mayo-ish (actually it can become almost jelly-like with enough spins around the mortar) you can stop adding the oil. Heed these words: if you add too much oil the *all i oli* will *break* and well... turn into another version of *all i oli* called, "Poc, but not poc enough." Just put it out anyway, and unless one of your guests is from the Baix Empordà they will never know and if they are they will probably give you a wink and a smile.
What's it taste like? Like garlic... and depending on the garlic you use (Spanish garlic, like Antonio Banderas, is small but *potente*), either strong to OMG! but texturally smooth and creamy. Leaving the goo to rest in a covered container in the refrigerator for twenty-four hours or so tends to cool things down. Some people are known to add a squirt of lemon juice.

OK, now let us move on to the Garlicy Mayonnaise version. Puristas… relax, turn away or leave the room, this has eggs in it. There are many versions of this and all require some form of power tool. Some use a $1200 Thermomix; some use a no name supermarket blender, but we are going to use one of those blenders on a stick gadgets or what is known in España as a "**MINIPIMER.**"

Let's call this "Juanjo's Insanely Easy *All i oli*." Listen, I know a really famous Spanish Chef is claiming this version as his invention but I am sorry "**REALLY FAMOUS SPANISH CHEF**" there are at least 20 Youtube videos of an assortment of Grandmas, Grandpas, truck drivers, small unattractive children and a German guy(!) making *all i oli* in exactly this way.

2	garlic cloves, peeled and sliced in half (feel free to experiment with this amount)
1	egg (at room temperature… I repeat, at room temperture…)
200 ml	(7 oz) mild extra virgin olive oil (many people use sunflower oil for this… you can too, or try a blend)
1/4	of a cuchara (teaspoon) of salt (as in the previous recipe, adjust to taste)
	a squeeze of lemon juice (or try the equivilent amount of a good white wine or sherry vinegar, or leave it out altogether)

JUANJO'S INSANELY EASY **VERSION**

1   Take the transparent, tube like blending bowl that came with your device and break an egg into it. Add the garlic, salt, lemon juice and the oil.

2   Plunge the blender into the ingredients all the way to the bottom of the blending tube. Set the blender's motor to high and hit the on switch. Keep an eye on the side of the tube to see when the miracle of emulsification transpires. Once a goodly portion has done its thing, move the blender slowly up and down the tube to finish the process. This should take not much more than a minute or so. And… thicker is better.

Small Plates:

THE MYSTERY OF THE
ESMOZARS DE FORQUILLA

Part of my due diligence for this book entailed sending Jordi's favorite recipes to a couple of great cooks: my friends Suzi Conklin and Sasha Kaplan. As always with Suzi and Sasha, I get a lot more back than I asked for. Suzi suggested that at the completion of writing and testing the recipes she would set up a couple of dinners whereby she would serve an appetizer, a soup, a side, and a main course, a salad, and dessert from the selected recipes. The suggestion made me think about how I have come to eat in my adopted homeland. Unless it's Thanksgiving, I just never eat in this structured sort of way. If I am fixing myself lunch I will make a simple dish and if I am ambitious I will add a salad. There are also some days where I just partake deeply in *cuina de llauna* (we'll get into this in a little later) and make a *torrada* (toasted open faced sandwich) from some spectacular Spanish tuna, a couple of strips of roasted peppers, a few strands of *cebollas confitadas*, a squirt of balsamic, and a sprinkle of good smoked sea salt, all of which come from various cans and glass vessels. I might toss on a few *arbequina* olives and chunks of *manchego* just to dress out the plate... but that, chicos, is lunch.

OK, I do add a *got de vi* and later I might walk over to any bar in the neighborhood and get a *tallat* (shot of espresso with a little milk, AKA a *cortado*) or a *helado* from the local grumpy *heladeria* (what is it about ice cream that makes a many ice cream vendors so irritable?) but generally it's more than enough to get me by.

The fact is, the vast majority of these dishes work well as a main or as a series of small plates, and that's pretty much how most people eat at Pinotxo. You eat small to medium-sized portions. You try a few things. You mix and match, and snag a perfect *navaja* off your neighbors plate while they are watching Juanito squeeze in a couple more customers. Your taste buds are happy. You don't have to waddle away stuffed to the gills and you may just live a little longer for it.

I suggest you try serving a couple of these recipes at a time. If you are going for something a bit more substantial, like an *estofada* or a *fricando,* just add a salad (either something leafy or one of the included composed varieties). You can always rev up the taste buds with some *embutidos*, some *queso oveja o cabra*, *aceitunas*, or a plato of *pimientos del padrón*. You can easily finish with some fresh fruit. Just remember in *cocina de abuela*, if you stress out during any part of the operation, either in the cooking or eating, then something is amiss. Remember, as paint can be your best value when it comes to remodeling, another glass of *vino tinto* with the right folks can completely transform a simple meal into a magnificent experience.

Thais' Grandma's
ROMESCO

It's the little differences here that drive you a bit loopy... But let us agree on this: *Romesco* is a sauce made from small and decidedly not fiery *nyora* peppers (which are red and about the size of an engorged golf ball), tomatoes, hazelnuts, almonds, garlic, parsley, fried, toasted or stale bread, a little red wine vinegar, olive oil, a little water and, finally, salt. Traditionally this is used as a dipping sauce when... how do I say this delicately... deep throating calçots. **CALÇOTS** are long and mild leek-like onions that are barbecued over construction debris and they are, a whole other story. Another sauce with exactly the same ingredients (except for the occasional addition of a couple of anchovies)is called "**XATÓ**" and goes on a dish also called "**XATÓ**" which is an amalgamation of escarole or belgian endive, walnuts, and or hazelnuts, olives, anchovies and *bacallà*. This dish is so important in the area just south of Barcelona that every year they crown a king and create a sort of road show tour competition called "**LA RUTA DE XATÓ**" where people from miles around come to taste and rate the offerings from the various *pobles*.

The thing is, try as you might to point out to some staunch Catalan foodistas that at least in some of the versions without the preserved fish, *salsa xató* and *salsa romesco* are exactly the same, they will deny it. Argue that both sauces are based on *nyora* peppers and share all the other ingredients and they will persist in their belief that they are different because *romesco* originally comes from Tarragona while *xató* comes from the Garraf *comarca*, (county, more or less), which is thirty miles to the north. Unless some sort of geomagnetic voodoo is having an effect, I hold that they are pretty much indistinguishable.

SO WHAT DO YOU DO WITH ROMESCO/SALSA DE XATÓ?

Well, as I mentioned earlier, *romesco*'s most famous pairing is with *calçots*. You sort of swat the thing around like Errol Flynn (which considering Errol's reputation could have a couple of meanings), flop it in a big dollop of sauce, slide it down your gullet and bite. It tastes wonderful and produces so much methane that if capturable, Catalunya would be the Saudi Arabia of self-produced natural gas. It's also great on fish, meat, grilled vegetables, eggs, and… pasta, which is in no way traditional, but who's checking at three in the morning when these kind of kitchen experiments are usually going down.

This recipe comes from my friend, Thais Tarrago Van Wijk, who just happens to be one of Spain's best entertainment lawyers and, as you can tell from her name, is both Catalan and Dutch. Obviously this comes from her Catalan side.

FES-HO TU

120 g	(4 oz) toasted almonds
3	dried *nyora* or *chorizero* peppers, soaked for at least 2 hours (See "Provisions", page 67)
1.5 kg	(3/4 lb) smallish, flavorful, ripe tomatoes cut in half lengthwise
1	head of garlic, unpeeled
1	clove of garlic, peeled and finely chopped
2	pieces of pan de pages (country loaf), well toasted
	extra virgin olive oil
	flakey sea salt
	water to thin

1 Remove the skins from the almonds.
2 Sprinkle the tomatoes with a little sea salt and place them on a baking sheet with the whole unpeeled garlic. Roast them for an hour in a 180° C / 350° F oven.
3 When done, remove the pulp from the tomatoes and reserve.
4 Cut the soaked peppers in half, remove the seeds, scrape pulp and reserve.
5 Grind the dry bread, almonds and chopped raw garlic in a food processor or use a mortar and pestle.
6 Once the baked garlic is cool enough to handle, dismantle the cloves and squeeze them into the food processor or the mortar, then add the tomato pulp and the meat of the pepper. Continuing to blend, adding just enough olive oil to make a smooth paste. Add water to thin out to a creamy consistency.

ESTOFAT DE VEDELLA

While prepping for these recipes, I was talking to my local *carnicero*, Esteve, about various and sundry things such as the importance of fat, tendons, and connective tissue, the exact location of the correct muscle for the right dish, and other minutia. In other words, all the things that add up to why Catalan and Spanish cooking tastes so damn good.

Eventually the conversation turned to a recap of our respective weekend activities. As many Barceloneses do, Esteve went to his "**POBLE**" (a village where the family has roots and a house or an apartment... considering that most everybody has one of these, this makes for a lot of *pobles* and gridlock most every Friday and Sunday evening) and had the traditional Sunday lunch with his relatives. Not yet having a "**MY OWN PRIVATE POBLE**" and, as is usually the case, I stayed in town and had a few friends over for dinner. We

For the *Sofregit*:

1	large onion, sliced thinly
2	cloves garlic, minced
1	red pepper, sliced into 1.5 cm (1/2 in) strips and then halved
2	medium tomatoes, grated using the secret Catalan grating technique and handshake (See "*El secret del tomàquet beneït*", page 76)
500 g	(1 lb) veal (1/2 leg and boneless shank), cut into chunks of about 4 cm (1.5 in). *Sis us plau...* don't go for the "lean and healthy" cuts... these will invariably be "dry and tasteless."
2	medium sized, peeled potatoes, halved and then quartered
4	cloves of garlic, whole and unpeeled
250 ml	(8 oz) of brandy
250 ml	(8 oz) of good, strong red wine
1	pre-made bouquet garni (or a few bay leaves and a couple of stalks of thyme, tarragon and rosemary)
	flour
	extra virgin olive oil
	salt
	freshly ground pepper

Optional:

	a handful of fresh or frozen peas
2	large carrots peeled and cut into 2.5 cm (1 inch) disks

1 Salt and pepper the meat and dredge it in flour.
2 In a deep cazuela (See "What's in a Pot, page 107"), fireproof casserole, or a dutch oven, add a couple of large splashes of olive oil, and over medium heat, brown the veal in small batches. The meat should be very, very rare on the inside.

made decidedly untraditional but surprisingly tasty sushi makis (I think the hit was my daughter's invention: Bacon, Philadelphia Cream Cheese, Carrot and Pistachio rolls. Like I said "**UNTRADITIONAL**" was the night's theme).

When I told Esteve about this, he somewhat sheepishly said that he'd never had Japanese food but would like to try it someday. Considering the fact that he's pushing fifty and has probably been in the food "**INDUSTRY**" since he was three or four, and that there are 1.6 million people in this naked city, many of whom are *estranjeros*, I was surprised that his culinary adventures were so cloistered. So I asked him what his favorite food was. His answer: "**WHAT YOU'RE COOKING, ESTOFADO!**" Lesson learned. You can take the Catalan out of Catalunya but know that they will always cross town for a good *croqueta* or a bowl of stew even though they've had it almost every week of their entire life.

After a few test rounds, I dropped a sample off for Esteve to try. I got two thumbs up, a "**MOLT BÉ**" and a "**VISCA CATALUNYA.**" Not bad for *guiri*... who was of course armed with the right recipe.

Serves 4 as a main course, more as a *tapa* or *platillo*.

3   Leaving the dripping and crumbly bits behind, remove the meat and reserve.

4   In the same cooking vessel, and using very low heat, and adding the ingredients sequentially, make a sofregit of the onions, garlic, red pepper, and tomatoes. (See "*Sofregit*", page 78)

5   When all is nice and soft return the meat to the cazuela.

6   Add the brandy and bring it to a boil. "Flame" the brandy and allow the flames to extinguish. Lower the heat to a simmer.

7   Add the wine and the bouquet garni or the loose herbs and return to a boil, then reduce the heat to an almost imperceptible simmer and cover. Let it percolate for at least 2 hours... or "xup xup" as they say here in Catalunya. Check occasionally and stir as needed. As with many of these one pot dishes, it's important not to add too much liquid as we are more or less braising and not boiling. The liquid should come up to the level of the ingredients or just below. The low heat and long cooking process will break down the tissues of the meat but leave the flavor and ultimately what makes it taste so good. If the brandy, wine, and the existing juices don't bring the liquid up to the right level, just add a little water.

8   Once the meat is very tender, add the potatoes and the optional carrots. When the potatoes are fork-tender you may, if you wish, add the optional peas. Cook for another 10 minutes or so then remove the bouquet garni or the loose herbs and voila! It's ready.

9   Salt and pepper to taste.

BÁSICOS

REDUCION OF BALSAMIC VINEGAR

The folks at Pinotxo are big fans of reduced Balsamic. They drizzle... dribble... squirt it on many things, and let's face it, why not? It (often in conjunction with flakey sea salt) tastes great and adds a welcome subtle, sweet and sour component to their lighter dishes.

Regarding reduced balsamic, you have a couple of options. You can buy "**ACETO BALSAMICO TRADIZIONALE**" which **1:** comes from the Italian regions of Modena and Reggio Emilia, **2:** is not even vinegar, (as it does not begin life as a mildly alcoholic fluid, but is made from unfermented grape juice... and special grape juice at that) and, **3:** is aged (and part of this is reduction by evaporation) in a succession of barrels of differing sizes and woods for anywhere from twelve to one hundred years. It has a stunningly complex flavor and one should, at least once in one's life, indulge in this lovely extravagance.

The other option is to make something like it yourself. Let's be clear: This is a lovely condiment and it "**TASTES REAL GOOD**" but it is not the real deal... so let's not call it anything like "**DIY ACETO BALSAMICO**" or "**LORRAINE'S QUICK AND EASY ACETO BALSAMICO**". Let's call it a "**REDUCTION OF STORE BOUGHT BALSAMIC VINEGAR.**"

Here's how to make it: Find a good quality Balsamico de Modena (this is the big batch stuff where they start with white wine vinegar and add things to it... you can tell by the ingredients and also by the limited amount of zeros on the price tag), and put it in a pan. Then allow it to simmer over a very low heat for as long as it takes to make a syrup of a consistency that makes you happy. Like I said, it's not bad at all, but it is in no way "**ACETO BALSAMICO TRADIZIONALE.**"

Seriously though, treat yourself to a bottle of the real deal and then begrudgingly dole it out to your favorite friends and family members. Proper stinginess can allow it to last for decades.

How do you apply it? If it's the reduced concoction give the dish a couple of licks from a squirty bottle. The real stuff... try an eye dropper.

VOLCANO BEANS

Bordering France between the mountains of Ripollès and the plains of the Empordà, the Garrotxa is a verdant *comarca* studded with forty dormant volcanos and people who will answer any question from many different languages in a profoundly staccato Catalan dialect that sounds to these untrained ears sort of like a Hungarian's first day trying to speak Italian. Beyond its fame as a former geologic hotspot, the area is known for its *farro* (cornmeal), *fajol* (buckwheat), truffles, *bolets* (mushrooms), snails, and perhaps most importantly, *els fesols de Santa Pau,* which take their name from a tiny medieval village whose surrounding fields have produced the tiny white beans for centuries.

Planting usually begins around the summer solstice, AKA *la nit de Sant Joan*, AKA midsummer's night, which is when all hell breaks out here in Spain; sins are purged, demons are chased away by flaming children, and Catalans sit on the beach until dawn drinking Estrella Damm beer (or more accurately Damn Estrella beer) and eating a God awful candied fruit infested cake called *coca de Sant Joan*. The nutrient rich volcanic soil makes the bean plants happy if the rain doesn't get them (*"Si no plou a Olot, no plou enlloc"*— "if it's not raining in Olot, it's not raining anywhere." Of course you know that Olot is the county seat).

The beans are then harvested, dried, beaten, selected, and put in cute little cloth bags by the second week of September. Repeat this process for eight hundred or so years and you too can produce perfect little beans that are thin skinned, not mealy, and flavorful enough that they are just fine on their own. Or scrambled with eggs. Or served with some *botifarras.* Or like this recipe, combined with baby calamari, a little flakey salt, and a squirt of reduced balsamic vinegar.

CALAMARSETS SALTATS AMB FESOLS DE SANTA PAU

Calamarsets, AKA "**CHIPIRONES**", AKA "**PUNTALLITAS**" (*en castellano*), AKA baby squid (*en ingles*). Call them what you will, this is one of those "**I CAN'T BELIEVE IT'S THAT SIMPLE**" recipes that truly represents the heart of Catalan cooking. It's just baby squid, small white beans, some salt, and a squirt of reduced balsamic vinegar.

There are only two things that are challenging about this recipe:

1

Cleaning the little
guys and…

2

Finding them
in Iowa.

Locating adult calamari is not much of a problem these days but finding the bambinos, well, that's potentially not going to be all that easy. In larger cities you would be wise to search out a giant Japanese or Asian supermarket. In the big *mundo del calamar* there are many sizes. What you want is the tiniest. Here it's like falling off a log… I just say "**CHIPPIES POR FAVOR!**" Sadly for you, it's not going to be that easy. Also check "**PROVISIONS**" (page 67) or a *"baby squid"* alert page on the website. One more thing. Yes, fresh would be best but frozen will do. And if you do use frozen… *por favor*, thaw them slowly in the refrigerator.

Finding **FESOLS DE SANTA PAU** will be a bit easier. You can either order them (again see "Provisions") or substitute navy beans… which, to be honest, are pretty darn close.

Serves 2. Like many of the recipes, this scales really well. More folks… just double up.

500 g (1 lb) *calamarsets (chipirones)*, cleaned
500 g (1 lb) *fesols de Santa Pau* cooked (See "Go Soak your Beans", page 144)
1 clove garlic, minced
2 sprigs parsley, minced
   reduced balsamic vinegar (See "Reduction of Balsamic Vinegar", page 93)
   extra virgin olive oil
   flakey sea salt, smoked if you can find it

1 Heat a wok to medium high temperature. (Yes, you can just use a skillet but a wok works great and it's what they use at Pinotxo).
2 Add a couple of tablespoons of olive oil and allow to heat up.
3 Add the garlic and after a moment (don't burn the garlic!) the cleaned *calamarsets* and stir with conviction. I know… you are looking at the eyes and the tentacles. Trust me, if you pitch these you will at some point karmically pay for your squeamishness. Toss them in… it's the best part. Once the last of the *calamarsets* have been added, wait a minute and then add the *fesols*, again keeping everything moving until all is warm and combined.
4 Serve with an artistic squirt of the reduced balsamic, a sprinkle of the parsley, and the smoked sea salt. Repeat as often as everyday.

TRUITA DE BACALLÀ

Ah, grandma's famous recipe for trout with salt cod… you will definitely be getting your vitamin D and Omega 3 here. Now, in Catalunya the word "**TRUITA**" has two meanings. One meaning is a kind of fish. The second meaning is a *tortilla*, which, in Spain, as you probably know, means a thick omelet-like affair and not a thin corn or wheat flour based crepe-like device as one might find in Mexico and/or Taco Bell. Catalan *tortillas* often deliciously deviate from the standard thick potato and onion variety that sits atop of the display case of just about every Bar Manolo on the peninsula.

Pinotxo's version, in keeping with the **NORMES I REGLAMENTS DE CATALUNYA,** skews more to the classic *tortilla francesa* (AKA an omelet), frittata side, and, in this recipe, we once again find ourselves exploring the intersection of *mar i muntanya*.

SERVES 1

- **2** eggs, beaten well
- **1** small piece of desalted *bacallà* to "al punto de sal" (a little salty…) shredded finely "by hand" (See "Baca… What?" page 98)
- **1/2** mild onion, sliced thinly
- **1** garlic clove, minced
- **2** sprigs of parsley, minced

    extra virgin olive oil

    a good flakey sea salt

    freshly ground pepper

1. Add some oil to a small skillet and make a *sofregit* of the onions (See "*Sofregit*", page 78). When the onions are nice and soft and have taken on some color, add the garlic. When this is cooked add the *bacallà*, (you want to just warm it through). Add the parsley at the last moment.

2. Add the *sofregit* to the beaten eggs and mix.

3. Wipe out the skillet you used for the *sofregit*, add a splash of olive oil, and coat the pan. Add the egg and the *sofregit* mixture and cook over low heat. Using your standard omelet technique, flip the *truita* anyway that you can. The center of the omelet should be soft and not overcooked.

4. Add a crack of pepper and a little sea salt if need be, and, if you wish, serve with *pan con tomate* (See "*Pa amb Tomàquet*", page 74).

    Hint: I have this great small skillet that has a modern, high quality non-stick coating. I know… I know… it's not traditional and wasn't handed down through the generations by my pilgrim forebearers. Look, trust me. Just get one. You won't believe how easy it makes things like this. It's so slippery.

Techniques AND Trucos

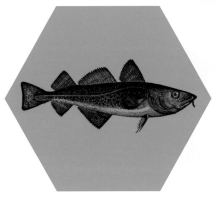

BACA... WHAT?

As you make your way through this book's recipes, you'll come upon much about the history and minutiae of the humble staple known as "salt cod". However, in sending out said recipes to our trusted, friendly cooks in the USA, we noticed something to be amiss; that being a certain discomfort with the idea of cod smothered, soaked and drowned in salt.

Let's break it down:

WHAT IS SALT COD?

It is the flesh of the Atlantic Cod (Gadus morhua). The fish is caught, gutted, cleaned, iced, and kept cold while at sea. Once back on land, it is split (opened up butterfly style) or divided into filets and cuts, and then brined. After two days, the fish is removed from the brine and dry salted in layers with ample salt separating the flesh of the fish. It is left to cure for eight to fourteen days. For a stronger flavor, the fish are left to cure for a longer time. The splits are often left to dry out further.

WHY NOT JUST USE UNSALTED COD?

Bacallà is really the Jamón Serrano of the sea. It's true that one can eat and enjoy uncured hams (and in Spain there are some lovely examples such as *Lacón* from Galicia and *Jamón Canario*) but it is truly a completely different experience. It's the same with fresh and salt cod. The curing process completely changes both the texture and the flavor of the meat in a truly extraordinary way. It may very well be the best fish you have ever tasted.

COUNTERFEIT SALT COD

The good news is that after decades, if not centuries, of over fishing Gadus Morhua is being taken off of the endangered list. The bad news is there is still a lot of fake *bacallà* out there. Made from more abundant fish like hake, ling, pollock, and haddock, the "fake" stuff may be fine for dishes like salt cod cakes and fritters (*buñuelos*) but for the recipes in this book you really need to hunt down the real thing.

DESALTING

Desalting is often perceived as a little mysterious but it's really simple. For your *bacallà* to be al "punto de sal" (at the just the right level of saltiness) take the cured fish (the cuts and sizes are described in the recipes) and submerge in cold water for two days or so. The water should be changed three times a day and the whole rig should be kept in the refrigerator. In a nutshell: soak fish forty-eight hours and change the water three times a day. That's it.

In Fernando Trueba's wonderful film, "**LA NIÑA DE TUS OJOS**", a troop of Spanish filmmakers leave Franco's Spain for Hitler's Germany to co-produce a film with the Nazis. Once installed in their hotel, the crew and actors are ecstatic to hear "**THAT THE OWNER KNOWS SPAIN...**" and that lentils are on the menu. Meanwhile, the director fumes about their utter disinterest in things like caviar and champagne. The fact is, most people on the Iberian penninsula know what they like; and what they like is more often than not absolutely terrific. Lentils, like *jamon* and *garbanzos*, are one of the fundamentals. This recipe, like *Calamarsets amb Fesols de Santa Pau* and *Remenat de Tallerinas*, represents the finest Mediterranean surf and turf tradition of "**MAR I MUNTANYA**"; brought into being by combining *coses de mar amb productes de la terra* (sea things with land things). In this case, the contrasting components are lentils, vegetables, *bacallà,* and eggs.

The verb *esqueixar* means "**TO TEAR**" and *esqueixada* means "**SHREDDED**" but it's also the name of a dish that features shredded *bacallà*, vegetables, and often a sprinkling of finely chopped or grated hard boiled eggs. Think then of this as a slightly vertical *esqueixada* with a lentil base, which is one of those little twists from the play book of Albert that he devised to make a set piece like this stand out.

Like the *Tonyina Escabetxada* (page 104), *Empedrat de Llenties Amb Bacalla* has roots in the Arabic pickled fish dish "**AHSEEKBA**", which, in turn, is a Catalan cousin of *ceviche*, whose origins are perhaps two thousand years old, and arrived in

EMPEDRAT DE LLENTIES AMB BACALLÀ

South America via the *conquistadores'* Arabic cooks: enslaved women from the recent "**RECONQUISTA**" of the formerly Islamic Spain "**AL ANDALUZ**", known to us now as Andalusia. So there you have it. A complete circle. An Arabic dish gone to the new world and then back again to the old, only to resurface slightly altered on a plate for you in Barcelona, or where ever you care to hang your tea towel.

200 g (8 oz) cooked lentils (See "Go Soak your Beans", page 144) You want them to be very slightly al dente, with each lentil distinguishable from every other lentil.

200 g (8 oz) skinless *bacallà* filets (See "Baca... what?", page 98)

2 green bell peppers, finely chopped

1 mild onion, finely chopped. Since the onions are raw, you should err on the side of the non-aggressive... walla wallas anyone? Even then, you might want to soak them ahead of time. A couple of hours in a solution of water and a little vinegar should do it.

1 large ripe tomato, finely chopped

2 hard boiled eggs, grated or finely chopped

A few black brine-cured olives with pits. No... not Missions, those tasteless little rubber rugby balls you stuck on your fingers when you were a kid. If you can't get *aceitunas negras de Aragón* then French Nicoise olives, although smaller, will get you pretty close.

freshly ground pepper

reduced balsamic vinegar (See "Reduction of Balsamic Vinegar", page 93)

extra virgin olive oil

a good flakey sea salt

Special cooking gadget: a few ring molds (8 cm/3 in)

1 Shred (*esqueixar*) the *bacallà* into strips with your hands and only your hands... OK, dainty rabble-rousers have been known to use a couple of forks. The finer the strips the better.

2 Place the mold on a serving plate... might I recommend a saucer?

3 Place a layer of lentils in bottom of the mold.

4 Add alternating layers of first the onions then the peppers, and finally the tomatoes.

5 Add another layer of the shredded *bacallà* and finally, if you so choose, grate a layer of the hard boiled egg on top of your creation. Many ring molds come with a little lid that is designed to compress the contents of the ring. If you have one, use it with a light touch.

6 Execute the unmolding process and serve with a squirt of the reduced balsamic vinegar, a crack of fresh pepper, a sprinkle of sea salt flakes, a couple of the black olives on the side, and if you are from España, a dribble of a high quality olive oil. *Mis amigos aqui* would put olive oil on ice cream if they had the chance.

EL REBOST:
CUINA DE LLAUNA
AND COSAS SECAS

Canned food has a bad reputation in the US. When I was a kid what came in cans was Dinty Moore Beef Stew and Franco American Spaghetti Os... "uh oh" is right. It didn't help that Dinty Moore's looked exactly like Gravy Train "Big'n Chunky" dog food.

But in other parts of the world food was canned for two reasons; harvests were bountiful and refrigerators and freezers were non-existent, rare, or just expensive and undependable thanks to a spotty electrical supply. In countries like Spain, the flavors created by the processes of canning and preserving (drying, salting, pickling) became part of the culinary esthetic. In fact, many preserved things are much more expensive than their fresh counterparts. Dry cured *jamón ibérico de bellota* (cured ham from the black-footed iberian pigs that free-range on acorns from the oak tree studded pastureland called a Dehesa) can cost 80€ a kilo if you are going in for the whole thing, and a lot more if you are asking your local *jamonista* to give you a hundred grams of hand carved *virutas* ("shingles", small, thin almost transparent slices). Fresh clams (*almejas*) always skew to the expensive side but put them in a can with a beautiful but slightly kitschy label and you can pay up to 50€ for 10 *almejas blancas* (white clams) from the Rias (estuaries) of Galicia. At 5€ a pop (that's over five clams... for a clam) you can be assured that they taste pretty damn good.

Conservas (canned goods) are considered so highly here that in Catalunya they have special times of the week and special places to eat them. Late Saturday or Sunday mornings is the traditional time to *"prendre un vermut"* at a bodega (a joint where you can buy wine in bottles or *a granel*, right from the cask as well as *conservas*), and have a *tapeo* (have a few small plates... *tapas* or *tapes* in Catalan) which can come exclusively from cans or be augmented by hot chow from a kitchen that is often the size of a broom closet. Note that in Catalunya a *vermut* (vermouth) is both a herb infused fortified wine and a weekend event which is supposed to be the prequel to a larger repast for family and friends. Note also that you can indeed have a *vermut* at a "vermut" but it's not obligatory... any beverage will do. Never let it be said that Iberians shy away from any opportunity to have a good time.

OK... go ahead and turn your nose up at creamed corn and Spaghetti Os but show a little respect for the big, wonderful, and delicious world of things in cans.

TONYINA ESCABETXADA

Another arabic import is *al-sikbaj* "**AHSEEKBA**", which mutates into "**EHSKABEH**" with a little tongue twisting.

"HEY SAMIR THIS IS REALLY GOOD, WHAT DID YOU CALL THIS? ESCABECH? QUE?"

Interesting also is that "**AL**" in arabic is a prefix meaning "**THE**". What is "the" in Castellano and Catalan? "**LA**" (*femenina*) or... "**EL**" (*masculino*). So in Arabic this breaks down to *al* (the) *sik* (vinegar), and *baj* (food). Which I think is pretty much of an "**IN THE POCKET**" description. Also, if you kind of peek at the word and concept sideways, you might "**GET**" that another of our recipes, *"Empedrat de Lenties amb Bacallà"* (page 100), is probably from the same culinary world.

Escabeche originally came into play to preserve an overabundance of food for times that were anything but overabundant. The process is more or less pickling. These days *escabeche* is more about flavor than long term storage but still, the longer you let things marinate (in the refrigerator, *si us plau*) the more tasty they will become.

So what kind of fish works for *al-sikbaj*? Oily fish. What kind of fish are oily fish? Pelagic fish, which for the most part means fish that are swimming around and not just hanging out on the bottom.

Bottom fish: Cod, flounder, sole, monk, etc.

Oily pelagic fish: Mackerel, sardines, anchovies, salmon, and in this case, tuna. *Ventresca de atún* comes from the belly, or the lower half of the fish. It's called "**TORO**" in Japanese and is the most oily part. Listen, you really don't have to use *ventresca* (it's the most expensive part of an already expensive fish) but it's what Jordi and clan Pinotxo often use, so for the sake of authenticity try to find some. But don't go crazy; "**LOMO**" (the loin, the upper half of the fish) in either steaks or pieces will work really well too.

500 g	(1 lb) tuna loin or ventresca (you can use smaller pieces as well)
4	medium onions, sliced thinly
2	peeled carrots, cut in to thin strips
1	pre-made bouquet garni or a combination of herbs like sage, dill, rosemary, thyme, and or bay leaves
1	full head of garlic cut in half laterally. Remove the skin from the top half. Keep the bottom half intact.
250 ml	(8 oz) extra virgin olive oil
250 ml	(8 oz) good white wine vinegar
125 ml	(4 oz) dry white wine
	a few fresh whole black peppers
1	teaspoon of your choice of *Pimentón de la Vera*, *dulce* or *picante*
	flakey sea salt
	Romaine lettuce (optional)

1   First, add a hearty pour of the olive oil to a skillet (or a cazuela), and using low heat make a… sofregit… really! Begin with the onions and when they become golden add the halved, peeled garlic cloves and carrots. Cook until the carrots are soft.

2   Add the other half of the garlic, the remaining liquid ingredients, and the spices. Bring to a boil and then reduce to a very, very low simmer, covered for 15 minutes. You are now extracting the flavors from the aromatic ingredients.

3   Add the tuna and again bring to a boil and then reduce to a very, very slow simmer, covered for another 15 minutes. You are now both slowly cooking the fish and coaxing the flavors of the aromatics into said fish.

4   Remove from the heat. Remove the bouquet garni if you used one (if you used loose herbs, leave them as they look rustic and homey) and allow to cool. Place everything in an airtight container and store in the refrigerator for at least 24 hours.

5   The remaining halved garlic cloves in the bottom half of the head of garlic can be removed and either eaten as is, or mashed and spread on toasted crusty bread. In fact, if you would like to add some of the tuna and the onions to said toasted crusty bread you will have made a torrada de escabeche, which is truly a lovely thing in its own right.

6   Serve at room temperature with a sprinkle of flakey sea salt and perhaps a leaf or two of Romaine lettuce on the side.

PERÒ…

Here's a little general insight about fish. When you are cooking fish and it turns "opaque" (meaning not in anyway translucent) it is cooked. Anything more is, depending on the fish, to either convert it into a building material or mush. In this dish the actual "cooking" part of this happened in the first few minutes. The long simmer is meant to infuse the fish with the flavors of the spices and to start the pickling process not to brickify it. *"Escabeche"* is a "pickled" cooked fish dish (and to be honest it doesn't have to be fish). *"Ceviche"*, although undoubtedly sharing a similar Arabic origin (and is equally as lovely) is raw "pickled" fish. They are however completely different dishes.

WHAT'S IN A POT

What would my desert island cooking gadget be?

1. A Ronco in Egg Scrambler?
2. An Electric pasta fork?
3. A Brookstone Grill Alert Talking Remote Meat Thermometer?
4. The Jordan Murphy designed Umbra iSPOON (a combination wooden spoon and Ipad stylus)?
5. Una cazuela de barro? (Translation: A mud casserole)

Yes, number five it is. We've mentioned this handy terracotta cooking vessel throughout this book but folks let me tell you one more time; if you want a durable, cheap, effective, and efficient cooking pot that looks like it was a prop from Sergio Leone's "The Good the Bad and the Ugly" then you must get yourself a *cazuela de barro.*

Yes, Bronwyn and Algernon, you could march yourself down to the nearest Williams Sonoma and shell out five C notes for a swanky Staube or Le Creuset cast iron cocotte, or you could shop where the *abuelas* shop, out in back of just about any *mercado* in Barcelona and get yourself a brick red "mud" *cazuela* for anywhere from one to six bucks… OK, a deep lidded one might set you back a tenner, but really, these babies, which come in a vast assortment of sizes, are your best cooking value. And they work like a charm.

"But it's just clay! And you put it directly on the fire?" Yes Gwyneth… you know what the heat shield for the Space Shuttle is made of? Ceramics. It's not made of French *bourgeois* cast iron. And if Le Creuset were all that concerned about heat why would they stick a cheap plastic knob on their lids (okay they recently switched to metal and Staubes have darling swappable metal handles shaped like adorable barnyard animals, reflecting I suppose what's in the pot?) Yes, you have to take a few precautions. You have to occasionally soak them in water and you should start your cooking session a little slower than usual, and if you are lucky (and smart) enough to have induction, it just won't work. But gas? Heck yeah. Electric? Bring it. Ovens… these guys were born and raised in ovens. Listen, you probably don't want to be doing any high temperature frying in one of these and in time (like years) they might eventually crack but you know what? You just fight your way through the Grandmas at the *mercado* and go lay down another fiver. Then you can use the cracked one for a rustic planter or fruit bowl. Check the provisions section (page 67) for where to obtain these items.

FAVES
A LA CATALANA

"...SOME FAVA BEANS AND A NICE CHIANTI."

One of the first things I stumbled onto here in Barcelona was Hannibal Lecter's favorite dish: *fava* beans.

We had just moved to Barcelona and my (then) much younger daughter and I were beginning what would become a weekly ritual: the Saturday morning trip to the local *mercado*.

We stopped by our usual *paradas*, gathering *embutidos* (ham and preserved meats), *frutos secos* (nuts and dried fruits), and *conservas* (olives, pickled and canned things), then had a *bikini* (grilled ham and cheese sandwich) at the bar. We saved the last stop for our favorite stand, Mercè del Prat. Run by an elderly brother and sister duo, the fruit and vegetable *parada* featured (and still features) produce from their *granja* (farm) in the nearby Delta del Prat. The *riu* Llobregat with the *riu* Besós, carve out the northern and southern borders of Barcelona. It's my favorite stop because the proprietors are just so sweet and the produce, although not exactly pretty, is the tastiest in the market. It's my daughter's favorite stop because they give her a bag of *mandarinas* and a couple of handfuls of *caramelos* (candies) as a gift because they like her.

Besides the super flavorful citrus, Mercè del Prat features seasonal produce from their farm, and on this visit, the *faves* had just arrived. *Faves*, plucked right off the bush, come in a long pod and at most stands that's how you buy them. Granted, shucking *fava* beans on your kitchen table while sipping a *vermut* on a Saturday afternoon is not exactly back breaking work but after you have experienced the novelty of this task for the twelfth time you might welcome the fact that Mercè del Prat has both a cute little shucking machine and a brother-in-law who runs it on the weekends. You hand him your intact pods and he gives you back a bag of fresh *faves* and a smile.

THIS IS ANOTHER CATALAN CLASSIC RECETA DE ABUELA. Usually, the first step of the recipe is to boil the fresh favas until they are tender. Pinotxo deviates from the norm by not putting the beans through this process and, to be honest, it improves the dish by adding a little snap.

You can, if you wish, serve this with a Chianti… but I don't recommend liver.

SERVES 4 AS A SIDE

750 g (1.5 lb) fresh fava beans

2 thick slices of bacon cut into 2 cm (1/2 in) strips

1 *botifarra negre* (morcilla) with the casing removed

1 bunch of garlic shoots, chopped fine

1 leek cut into 2 cm (1/2 in) rounds

1 wine glass (250 ml) of white semi sweet wine, sweet sherry or moscatel

1 ripe tomato, grated (See "*El secret del tomàquet beneït*", page 76)

1 dried bay leaf

1 small bunch of mint, chopped coarsely
extra virgin olive oil
salt to taste

1 In a skillet or a *cazuela*, fry the bacon in a little splash of olive oil and then crumble in the sausage. Reserve.

2 In the same pan *sofregiu* (remember, fry slowly over a low heat) the vegetables, mint, and bay leaf. When everything is soft, add the tomato.

3 Add the favas and when they have "taken on some color" return the bacon and crumble the morcilla into the pan.

4 Using the tried and true braising technique, add the wine, and if needed, just enough water to cover all the ingredients no more than halfway.

5 Cover and cook over a low heat for about 20 minutes. If you like a thicker "potage", as I do, leave the cover off for the last 10 minutes. Contrary to every other version of this recipe, try to leave the favas a little bit *al dente*.

REMENAT de TALLARINES

Mar i Muntanya. The sea and the mountains, surf and turf... call it what you will, but the Catalans are famous for combining sea critters with land critters. In this recipe it's more "**MAR I BARNYARD**" and is so simple, quick to make, and tasty that you might find yourself waking up in the middle of the night to fix some. That is, of course, if you have fresh clams on hand.

As Jordi says, "**GOOD FOOD COMES FROM POOR CULTURES... A RICH CULTURE HAS EVERYTHING THEY WANT BUT THOSE WITH LESS HAVE TO GET BY, REFINE, REUSE AND MAKE THE BEST OUT OF SIMPLE INGREDIENTS**". Like the vast majority of Spanish and Catalan dishes, it's the simplicity of the technique and the quality of the ingredients that make this dish so magical, so sensuous, so tasty, and in this case, a little bit... dirty. This is one of my favorites.

SERVES 2 AS AN ENTREE, MORE AS A TAPA OR PLATILLO

300 g (10 oz) of really fresh *tallerinas* (these are very small clams but slightly bigger ones work fine too OK... small steamers... no geoducks!)

50 g (2 oz) of thinly sliced mild onions

3 high quality, free-range eggs from very happy chickens

extra virgin olive oil

sea salt flakes

twist of freshly ground black pepper or a dusting of *Pimentón de la Vera*

Secret cooking tool: 1 glass pan lid... and it has to be glass because you have to see what's going on deep inside the pleasure dome. Jordi and company put the clams directly on the griddle and use an old pyrex bread *pan*. They also have a quarter inch of calluses on their fingers. Trust me, use the pan lid.

1 Beat the eggs well.
2 Pre-heat a skillet to medium...relax, no matter what you do, it will come out really tasty...unless you go for a half hour jog while it's cooking. Add the olive oil. After a second or two, lower the heat and saute the onions very slowly until golden. Remove the onions and add them to the beaten eggs.
3 Toss in a little more oil and add the tallerinas. Now quickly cover the pan with the aforementioned glass pan lid (you are in effect making a steamer). Pay close attention. You'll notice that in a short while the tallerinas will open and release this amazing sea juice that was trapped inside their shells.

4   Once all the clams have opened (and this is the tricky part because you want as many of them as possible to open but you also don't want all the juice to evaporate), remove the lid and toss in the egg and onion mixture then lightly oscillate everything with a wooden spoon.

5   Cover the pan and watch closely. Once the eggs are just "cooked" (and by this I mean they have just turned opaque), switch off the heat. The residual temperature of the pan and the clams will finish cooking the eggs.

6   Slide the eggs and the clams (which have now become one, more or less) into shallow bowls. Add a sprinkle of the salt flakes, a crack of pepper and/or a very light dusting of the *pimentón*, and serve while it's still warm.

"Now how do I eat this?"

Another aspect of life in Iberia is that people here are not afraid to touch each other, things, and food... both theirs and that technically belonging to others. When they cook, they dive in with both hands, fingers as naked as the day they arrived in this odd and beautiful place. Poking, squeezing, wiping, tasting... sometimes licking. Here, when it comes to microbes, it's the more the merrier and considering that Spain has one of the healthiest populations in Europe, it must be working.

Right. "But how do I eat this?"

Undoubtedly, you will start by picking the clams out of their shells with your fork... and you might just stab an errant chunk of briny egg. Soon you'll realize that much of the egg is stuck to the shell and ultimately to the meat of the clam. The residual heat has melded the molecules (egg, shell, and clam meat) together pretty damn well. What are you going to do? Go for the low hanging fruit? The big chunks? The easy pickings... and leave the rest on the plate? Come on now. You're not one of those people who leave pizza bones behind are you? This plan of attack may be the correct and tidy thing to do but you'll miss out on all of the good stuff and ultimately risk leaving the table hungry and frustrated. Give up and give in. Put down that fork, grab one of those tiny mollusks, spread the shells apart, stick out your tongue and get down to business. Obviously, I could get really descriptive about all things sea-like, and oh-so salty; about the firm, rigid texture of the clams and how this contrasts with the warm, soft, suppleness of the eggs, and how you have to use your tongue and your teeth to scrape said eggs off the rock hard shells... and how this seems oh-so beautiful and yet, at the same time, oh-so obscene and transgressive and yet...and yet just oh-so right. But I shan't... I shall leave some things up to your imagination.

In other words, just go for it.

REMENAT DE GAMBES

3	raw large shrimp; beheaded, peeled, deveined, and split in two lengthwise
2	alls tendres (AKA spring garlic or garlic shoots), coarsely chopped
50 g	(2 oz) *trompetas de la mort* (or another strong flavored wild mushroom... chanterelles for example)
100 g	(4 oz) zucchini sliced into 3mm (1/8 in) disks
3	medium sized asparagus (this is not very critical; if you love asparagus use more). Discard the woody part, snap off the tips, and slice the rest into 6mm (1/4 in) chunks.
1	large egg
	extra virgin olive oil
	flakey sea salt (smoked works great)
	freshly ground pepper
	Pimentón de la Vera (optional)

Remenats, *revueltos*, scrambled eggs... I think the elegant simplicity of these dishes says a lot about how most Catalans look at life. So when it comes to your super fresh shrimp, your straight-from-the-farm asparagus, garlic shoots, and zucchini, leave them alone. Lay off those foraged mushrooms and your eggs from happy, free-range chickens with names like Marta and Montse. Keep these elaborate, over-worked extravaganzas for less tasty recipes. As this humble dish shows, most of the time simple is best. Give it a try and let it be a base for your future excursions into the essential.

The great thing about this dish is that it scales wonderfully. Below, you will find the ingredients for one person. Got company? Just multiply.

1. Saute the asparagus slices and tips, and the zucchini, in olive oil until soft. Remove and reserve.
2. In the same pan (add olive oil as needed) saute the mushrooms. When cooked, remove and add to the reserved vegetables.
3. Still in the same pan, add the garlic shoots. When wilted, add the shrimp and saute until they are just cooked through.
4. Return the vegetables and the mushrooms to the pan and continue to stir until they are warmed through. Toss in the egg or eggs, as the case may be. Remenats or revueltos are usually broken directly into the pan and then stirred about until just cooked through. Do this.
5. Add a sprinkle of salt and the pepper at the moment they are served. You may, if you wish, add a dusting of *Pimentón de la vera* of either the *picante* or *dulce* variety. I love this stuff and usually only restrain myself from using it on things like apple pie and hot cocoa.

PEKING DUCK

Peking duck? Wha? It's like those Cuban Chinese restaurants on the upper west side of Manhattan... visions of recent Chinese immigrants running vast empires of bric-a-brac shops by day and slammin' daiquiris and mojitos, scraping plates clean of *ropa vieja,* and dancing the Mambo by night. I have always loved culinary incongruity. Well, this is not quite that but it does represent how food can be such a wonderful medium of cultural exchange. It also points out how working the food trade is less of a "**JOB**" and more of a calling.

The story behind this story begins like this: María José, Jordi, and Albert became friends with José María Kao who is the chef and, along with his brother Luis, owns "Shanghai" which has its origins in Restaurante "El Peking." This restaurant was started by their father, Kao Tse Chien, who immigrated from Taiwan to serve as chef at "El Gran Dragon" which was Barcelona's first Chinese restaurant. The always inquisitive Albert became enamored with the house specialty, *Pato Pekin* ("**ÀNEC LACAT**" in Catalan) and, as was his way, decided to create a version of it for Pinotxo. No, you don't make a duck balloon by blowing up the skin with a bicycle pump like in the classic recipe but if Chef Kao approves you know it has to be good.

1	smallish duck, like around 1.8 kg (4 lb)
2	pieces of star anise
	salt and pepper

For the orange, ginger, and soy sauce

2	cups of orange juice (fresh squeezed is best, filter out the pulp)
170 g	(3/4 cup) brown sugar
1	small knob of ginger, grated
3	tablespoons of good quality soy sauce

Special cooking gadgets

a *freidora* (a deep fryer, see "Ode to a *Freidora*", page 127)

a squeezy bottle

BE FOREWARNED: THIS TAKES A LITTLE BIT OF PREP TIME.

1. To dry out the skin, leave the duck in the refrigerator uncovered for 24 hours
2. Preheat oven to 220° C / 425° F
3. Salt and pepper the duck inside and out, and place the star anise inside the body cavity.
4. You might as well make the sauce while you are waiting for the oven to come up to temperature. Add the orange juice to a saucepan and bring to a boil.
5. Add the sliced ginger to the orange juice. Reduce to simmer and cook for 15 minutes. Remove the ginger.

6   Add the brown sugar and return to a boil. Lower the heat to a simmer, reducing the sauce by 50%.

7   Weigh your duck. Figuring 20 minutes per 500 g (1 lb), divide the cooking time by 3. For example a 1.8 kg (4 lb) duck will take 160 minutes to cook in 3 passes of 53 minutes.

8   Place duck, breast side up, in a roasting pan (if you have a roasting rack all the better) for the first interval.

9   At the end of the first interval, and with as much grace, safety, and savoir faire as possible, flip the duck, back side up and continue to roast for the second interval.

10 After the second interval has passed, flip the duck back to breast side up and continue for the final interval.

11 If you have an instant reading thermometer check the thickest part of the thigh (without touching a bone). 75º C / 165º F is perfect for this recipe.

12 Remove the duck and let it cool. Cut into serving size portions. Pinotxo divides their duck into 4 pieces, 2 winged breasts and a 2 leg and thigh combos. And please save the rendered duck fat for the most amazingly crispy and tasty fried potatoes you will ever have. Yes, this is more French than Iberian but who's counting?

13 OK, final step. Preheat your *freidora* to 180º C / 350º F and then, a few portions at a time, crisp up the duck skin by frying the pieces for around 20 to 30 seconds.

14 Plate the portions. Taking your handy squirty bottle which you have preloaded with orange soy ginger sauce, artistically and liberally apply it to the duck and underlying plate.

DUCK, DUCK, PATO?

Jordi:
"Albert, Maria Jose, and I were having dinner at our friend Jose Maria Kao's restaurant "Shanghai.""

"Albert being Albert , he went to the kitchen and asked them how they did things. So one thing led to another and we started doing Peking Duck at Pinotxo. We love this dish. One day Jose Maria came in and said that ours is better than his!"

FOR A FEW OLLAS MORE

Spain has great people, great food, and great cookware... OK I could have said music, cities, castles, mountains beachs... but I picked cookware? Yep, I picked cookware.

Look, you got much praised *cazuela*, the brilliantly utilitarian and beautiful *paella*, and then there is the lovely stuff that I have come to call "enamelware" or en Castellano *"utensilios de cocina esmaltada."* It's that speckled metal stuff that you saw around the campfire in every black and white cowboy movie. You know, John Wayne or Randolph Scott would hunker down near the fire and pour themselves a cup of steaming "joe" from a speckled metal coffee pot into a speckled metal coffee mug. They would blow, take a sip, grimace, and then pour the contents into the fire. Terse dialogue would ensue between John or Randolph and Gabby Hayes regarding the quality of the coffee which would lead to Hayes saying, "Dadgummit!" and exiting stage right in a huff. It's that stuff and it's great. Beyond coffee pots and mugs there are skillets (*sartenes*), ollas (*pots*), sauce pans (*sartenes hondas*) with handles (*con mango*) or without and of course *paellas*. I love my *"utensilios de cocina esmaltada"* and so will you. Check "Provisions" on page 67, for where to buy these classics.

Within Pinotxo's roster of extraordinary dishes there are a few that stand out as the rockstars of the menu. *Cigrons amb botifarra negra i ceba* is one of them. And, like all of Pinotxo's best recipes, it's dead simple, owing much of its magic to the quality of its ingredients.

In this case, the dominant flavor comes from the spices in the sausage and a little Albert magic in the use of Argentinian *Chimichurri* spice mix. The *botifarra negra (morcilla en castellano)* that Pinotxo uses, perhaps reflecting Spain's seven hundred years of Islamic rule, has more than a hint of North African spices and cinnamon. Yes, the sausages are pork... let's just call it a slightly ironic cultural contrast.

500 g (1 lb) garbanzo beans cooked (See "Go Soak your Beans", page 144)

1 *botifarra negra (morcilla)*, skin removed

2 onions, sliced finely

a palm full of raisins

a palm full of pine nuts

1 clove of garlic, minced

2 sprigs of parsley, minced

1 hefty teaspoon of *Chimichurri* spice mix (See "Provisions", page 67)

flakey sea salt

extra virgin olive oil

1. Add the pine nuts to a medium-sized skillet and toast over medium heat until they are just beginning to turn golden. Be careful, as they can go from golden brown to golden black in a very short amount of time. Being lazy, I usually just toast one side. Remove from the pan.
2. *Sofregir* the onions in a hearty squirt of olive oil over medium heat. (See "*Sofregit*", page 78)
3. When the onions are transparent and on the golden side, add first the *chimichurri* blend and then after a moment the pine nuts and the raisins.
4. Crumble in the morcilla. Stir and chop often and diligently until the morcilla is cooked through. Pinotxo uses a dedicated paint scraper for this operation and so could you.
5. Add the garbanzos. Gently stir until the garbanzos are warmed through.
6. Sprinkle on the parsley and serve with little extra virgin olive oil and a dash of the flakey sea salt.

Pollastre
A LA CATALANA

There is definitely a medieval hit to some of these dishes. This is one of those. Perhaps it's the sweetness of the dried plums and apricots aligned with the savoriness of the long braised chicken. For some reason, **THE COMBINATION OF FLAVORS AND TEXTURES REMINDS ME OF CHRISTMAS**. But that is yet another story.

SERVES
8

1 Soak the plums and apricots in the brandy for at least 2 hours.
2 Over medium heat, toast the pine nuts in a skillet until they are just golden. Be careful, they burn easily. Reserve.
3 Add a hearty pour of olive oil to a *cazuela or a deep pot* and fry the chicken over medium heat. Turn the chicken so that all sides are golden brown. Remove.
4 Add the bacon, and when cooked on the crispy side, reduce the heat, add the onions, and cook slowly until golden.
5 Add the chicken, plums, and apricots. Toss in the brandy in which the dried fruit was soaking and flame it.
6 After the flames have extinguished, add the grated tomatoes, garlic, and the bouquet garni or loose herbs.
7 Add the white wine, and if required, just enough stock to cover the chicken no more than halfway. Less is more. Cover and let simmer over very low heat for at least an hour. Hint: 2 hours or more of braising will only make the dish more tasty… take as long as you want, it only gets better. (See *"Braise Moi"*, page 150)
8 Just before serving, if you used the bouquet garni, remove it and sprinkle on the pine nuts.
9 Salt and pepper to taste.

1 medium sized, high quality, free-range chicken, cut into 8 pieces
3 mild onions, chopped coarsely
1 head of garlic, separated into cloves. Leave half unpeeled, and peel and mince the rest
2 tomatoes, grated, using the secret Catalan grating technique and handshake (See *"El Secret del Tomàquet Beneïda"*, page 76)
1 pre-made bouquet garni (or a few bay leaves and a mixture of stalks of dried thyme, tarragon, and rosemary)
6 dried plums
4 dried apricots
100 g (3 oz) pine nuts
1 2.5 cm (1 in) slice of smoked bacon cut into *"dados"*, 1.5 cm (1/2 in) strips
250 ml (8 oz)) dry white wine
250 ml (8 oz) brandy
250 ml (8 oz) poultry stock (See "It's the *Caldo*", page 136)
   The quantity may vary depending on the size of the chicken, see instructions to the left.

   extra virgin olive oil

   salt and fresh ground pepper to taste

FRICANDÓ
AMB
MOXERNONS

Meat imperialism? The world does not have a UN charter in place regarding how one should and should not cut up animals; and if you guessed that in Spain they do it differently, you'd be correct. Take, for example, the cut used in *Fricandó*. Again, according to my *carnicero* Esteve, the cut for a *fricandó* always comes from the **LLATA**. No, a *llata* is not a plastic car from the former Soviet Union. It's a muscle that sits on top of the shoulder of a cow and in the anglo-saxon world falls into what makes up part of the chuck. Apparently our world now has become hip to this cut and have christened it "**SHOULDER TENDERLOIN**", and undoubtedly raised the price by at least half.

The first thing you are going to have to is find a real butcher who can get you this cut and frankly it won't really be a *fricandó* without it. Why? Esteve explained that there is a nerve that runs down the center of the cut which serves to further keep the meat juicy and tender as it breaks down in the braising process. There you have it. Now hunt one down. The other requirement is the addition of dried "**MOIXERNON**" mushrooms. Yes, you guessed correctly, this is our old friend "**CALOCYBE GAMBOSA**", known apparently in English as St. George's mushroom. You can use other dried mushrooms but if you are aiming for the full Pinotxo experience you should try to find these. What is non-negotiable though is that you really need to use dried mushrooms... Fresh just won't cut it. The flavor and texture are just right for this dish, which by the way has been around since the Romans.

SERVES 4 OR MORE AS A TAPAS OR A "PLATILLO"

8	1.5 cm (1/2 in) slices of veal shoulder tenderloin
50 g	(2 oz) dried moixernon mushrooms (See "Provisions", page 67)
2	onions, sliced thinly
2	garlic cloves, minced
1	tomato peeled, seeded and grated (See "*El secret del tomàquet beneït*", page 76)
	high quality veal or beef stock (See "It's the Caldo", page 136)
1/2	teaspoon of nutmeg
1	tablespoon cocoa powder(dutch process if available)
1	teaspoon *Pimentón de la Vera, picante*
	white wine
	flour
	extra virgin olive oil
	salt and freshly ground pepper to taste

1. Soak the moixernons for at least 2 hours, then drain through a fine sieve. These mushrooms often come with a little Catalan dirt. This may seem sort of mystical but is in reality just unpleasantly crunchy unless you remove it.
2. Salt and pepper the meat and then dredge it in flour.
3. In a *cazuela*, a heavy, lidded skillet or a dutch oven, brown the meat and reserve. (See "What's in a Pot", page 107)
4. Add a splash of olive oil to your chosen cooking vessel, and over low heat, saute the onions, the garlic, and the moixernons (add more oil if you need to). When the onions are translucent, add the grated tomatoes, the cocoa, the *pimentón*, the nutmeg, and a hearty dash of white wine.
5. When everything is nice and soft, return the meat and add enough beef stock to just cover the ingredients. Bring to a boil, cover, and reduce to a very low simmer for at least an hour and half.
6. Remove the lid for the last half hour to reduce the *salsa*.
7. Salt and pepper to taste and perhaps serve with *Fesols de Santa Pau* or white rice.

SUQUET *de rap*

I remember my first *suquet*. It was a wonderful, enlightening amalgamation of perfectly cooked fish, an intense broth, and potatoes infused with the flavors of the fish and the cooking liquid.

Like the Minorcan *Caldreta*, a *suquet* is another "**FISHERMAN'S DISH**" that originated from the need to eat simply, cheaply, and most of all, well, while still at sea. A fish is caught. A stock is made from the less pretty parts. The stock is strained, potatoes and the prettier parts of the fish are added, and the whole thing is cooked through. Dinner is served.

Like many recipes in Spain and Catalunya, it's all about the quality of the ingredients. In this case, the most important component is the fumet, or fish stock.

Here in Barcelona we are blessed with pescaderias where the proprietors actually do more than unload and set out pre-packaged styrofoam containers. They are there to help, advise, offer tips, recipes, and their highly evolved skills, which in the case of pescaderos and carniceros, are really more akin to those of surgeons.

Here they help you select and dress the fish to your specifications.

It goes like this. I tell Pedro, my friendly neighborhood pescadero, that I'm going to make a rap (monkfish) suquet. His first question is, "how many people?" I answer, "Four. No kids." He plucks a medium size fish, fresh looking if not exactly handsome, from its bed of ice. He holds it up and points the head directly at me. Like always, I say, "Ah, OK. gimme Peter Lorre." Like always he doesn't understand. You see, to me the head of a monkfish looks a lot like Peter Lorre. Or Edward G. Robinson. Or J. Edgar Hoover. Or Roy Cohn. Pedro sets to it, brandishing a big, fierce-looking blade, the kind of knife pescaderos and pescaderas use to seemingly do everything from delicately separating filets from paper thin skin to decapitation, which is what he ultimately has in mind for poor Herr Lorre. First though, comes the evisceration.

An incision is made and all the inedible internal organs are removed. As I watch, my fish is converted into 4 steaks, a head and a tail. Pedro gifts me a merluza head and spine to round out the last two ingredients for the fumet. I hand over my credit card and Pedro hands me back a bag containing two packages; one with the pretty parts and the other with the gorey bits that are headed for the stock pot. As I take the bag, I comment on the freshness of the turbot. Pedro smiles and says that though admiration is great, it would be even better if I took one home. What is a market without banter?

You should try to find a fishmonger who can give you this level of service because, truth be told, neither you nor I are very accomplished fish surgeons. Besides, it just makes things so much easier.

The other great thing about this dish is that we get the opportunity to try out our chops at making yet another mysterious fundamental of Catalan cooking, the picada.

1   whole monkfish 1.5 kg (3 lb) cleaned and cut into 4 cm (1.5 in) steaks. Save the head for the *fumet,* if you can acquire another head or two by all means do.

potatoes, peeled and sliced into 1.5 cm (1/2 in) disks

1   liter (1 qt) *fumet* (recipe follows)

picada (See "*Picada*", page 80)

For the *fumet*:

The head of the monkfish (and hopefully another noggin and spine or two)

2   ripe tomatoes, grated (See "*El secret del tomàquet beneït*", page 76)

1   celery stalk cut into 1.5 cm (1/2 in) pieces

1   small bunch of fennel leaves, chopped finely

A small palm full of whole black peppercorns (around 12 or so)

1   leek (including most of the greens) chopped into 3 cm (1 in) disks

salt to taste

Make the fumet

1   Place the head of fish (and what ever other unwanted fish parts you have been able to wrangle), along with the vegetables, in a *cazuela* or a deep pot. Cover with water and bring to boil and then reduce to a low simmer for ninety minutes or so. The longer you simmer the more intense the flavor.

2   Pass the liquid through a fine strainer and discard the solids.

3   Return the liquid to the *cazuela*, bring to a low boil and reduce the liquid by a third. Salt to taste.

And then

1   Add the *picada* to the simmering *fumet* after it has reduced by a third or so.

2   Add the potatoes. When they are just fork tender...

3   Place the fish on top of the potatoes. Cover the pot. When the fish is "just" opaque (depending on the thickness of the steaks this should take around 5 minutes) remove from the heat and let the dish rest for ten minutes.

4   If you wish serve with "*All i oli.*" (See *All i oli*, page 84)

ODE TO A FREIDORA

Fear fat not and remember that ham in Spain is considered a vegetable.

Found in five star molecular research facilities and every *Patata Bravas* slinging Bar Manolo from Punta de Estaca de Bares in Galicia to Punta de Tarifa in Andalusia, the *friedora*... or as we so crudely put it in English, "The Deep Fat Fryer" is a really bigger player in *cocina española*. I shall not go into too much depth regard this near universal technique (again we seemingly have our Arab friends to thank for this) but I will say that, if done with a modicum of care, "deep frying" will not contribute any more additional fat than frying in a shallow pan. Nothing else can make things like wispy tempura, hearty croquetas, unassumingly vegan falafels, and yes Mars Bars, so crunchy.

Do you have to use a *friedora*? No, all you really need is a pot, some vegetable oil, an instant read thermometer to tell you when you are up to temperature, and some tongs or a skimmer to both immerse and remove the crispy chow but... a deep fat fryer makes this all much safer, less messy and accurate. Go forth and make peace with your new falsely maligned friend.

C od… or to be more specific, dried cod… Books have been written about it. Wars have been fought over it with the maps to the fishing spots hidden away like plans for nuclear weaponry. Salt cod was the ultimate storable commodity. Cod has been caught, salted, and dried by the Basques, Portuguese, and the Scandinavians for over five hundred years.

Two things have contributed to making salt cod, *bacalhau*, *bacalao*, *bacallà*, *klipfisk*, *morue salé* or *makayabu* trendy; the near-complete extinction of the grand bank shoals by aggressive overfishing in the seventies and eighties, and the discovery of this formerly low-rent staple by hip, young chefs. Absence makes the heart, and apparently, the stomach, grow fonder but foodie fickleness has nothing to do with what's really going on in southern Europe regarding this delicious fish. Cod; salted and dried from a finny wonder to a rock-like slab that looks like one of the embryonic stages of the Alien, still tastes as good now as it did half a millenia ago.

Here in Barcelona I can just go to my friendly *bacallà* man or lady in any *mercado* and they will hand over the fish already soaked and desalinated to a "**PUNTO DE SAL**." Which basically means at a "**JUST RIGHT**" level of saltiness. In your neck of the woods chances are you might not be so lucky. If that's the case, go immediately to "Baca… What?" (page, 98) for the full low down. Also check out "Provisions" (page, 67) for sources.

Here's a dead simple recipe that, in addition to being tasty, is actually quite lovely looking.

Bacallà
AMB
CEBA I PEBROT VERD
CONFITATS

500 g (1 lb) desalinated and re-hydrated *bacallà* filets cut into approximately 7 cm x 10 cm (3 x 4 in) pieces. Optimally, you want the pieces to be at least 4 cm (1.5 in) thick (See "Baca... What?", page 98)

2 medium mild onions, sliced thinly

1 green bell pepper or 2 "Italian" peppers, sliced thinly into strips (See "The Problem with Peppers", on the following page.)

a hefty teaspoon of sugar

extra virgin olive oil

freshly ground pepper

1 First, make a *sofregit* of the onions. I swear Catalan ice cream or *pastel de chocolate* (chocolate cake) must begin with moving onions around in a pan for at least a half an hour. OK no whining. Get out your favorite wooden spoon, put on your favorite recording of the Cobla de Vilafranca, add a couple of tablespoons (AKA a hearty dollop) of olive oil to a skillet, and stir those onions over low heat. Resist the temptation to crank it up and get'er done. *Lento, lento, lento.*

2 Once the onions have begun to turn transparent, add the sugar, which will help caramelize the onions and turn them the color of straw. I know, sugar… trust me. All will be made clear shortly.

3 Add the peppers and cook them until you think they are too are soft. This will take a while and remember, low and slow is the way. Take your time. If you are in a hurry, cover the pan and let it braise away. Once all is soft and harmonious (with these kind of dishes *al dente* is really not part of the vernacular), transfer the vegetables to your serving dish.

4 Add another pour of olive oil, and once it's hot, add the fish. After a couple of minutes, flip the pieces and then continue to cook for another few minutes. "Doneness" in fish is sort of a personal affair but for me, unless I am doing the seared tuna thing, once the fish is opaque it's done… no more, no less. However, in the case of *bacallà*, it's already almost opaque even before you cook it. I find that *bacallà* is done when the segments of the flesh separate easily.

5 Place the fish on the bed of onions and peppers. Hit it with a crack of fresh pepper. You won't need salt. Dig in and see how the subtle sweetness of the peppers and onions complements the round saltiness of the fish. *Molt be!*

THE PROBLEM WITH PEPPERS

So here in España it's not like there are dozens of varieties of fresh peppers (the myriad of dried capsicums is another story). There 's your standard "bell" which can be substantial in size, is most often red, less often green, and more or less never yellow. The tapa favorite, the pequillo from the Navarra region in Northern Spain, is bright red, mild, cone shaped and usually roasted, canned, and stuffed with everything from tuna to cream cheese. Also tapa fodder is the small, green *Pimiento del Padrón* which originally only came from the pueblo of Padrón in Galicia. Given a large enough batch of these peppers, you'll often times come upon the occasional, slightly spicy mutant (but listening to the Iberians you would think that one out of ten was a *habanero*). These are always prepared *a la plancha* with a manly (or womanly) whack of salt. But today's troublesome item is a long, slightly skinny number which looks just like an Anaheim but is definitely not an Anaheim. Here they are usually just called *pimientos verdes* but I have come to find out that in *guiri* land they are generally known as "Italian" peppers. Like I said, they look a lot like Anaheims but their skin is less tough and they are missing that slightly bitter aftertaste. In Italy they go by the name of *Frigitelli*. If you can find them please use them, if you can't then your next option is to use standard issue green bell peppers... they are close enough. *Jalapeños*... on the other hand. are not.

TRINXAT DE LA **CERDANYA**

AH WINTER!

In Barcelona you can tell that winter is coming because people start to wear socks. OK… winters are generally mild here but just up the road in the region of Cerdanya it's a different story.

Straddling the border of France and Spain, the region is split down the middle by the Pyrenees. Granted, the Pyrenees are not the Alps; not in height or ruggedness or grandeur or throngs of tourists riding cable cars from peak to peak, but for me they feel homey and human… like they have been respectfully shared by man and nature for a very long time. The food from the region is simple, tasty, and as is often the case in mountainous regions, a bit on the robust side.

Trinxat, (which means "**SLICED**" or "**CHOPPED**" in Catalan) is probably the most emblematic dish of the region and again combines what is available in simple and really tasty ways.

Feel free to reduce the recipe proportionally if you have not single-handedly brought the herd down from the high pasture.

1 small to medium winter cabbage, tough outer leaves removed, cut into quarters

1 kg (2 lb) of firm potatoes peeled, halved and then quartered

2 1.5 cm (1/2 in) slices of *Cansalada viada* cut into 10 cm (2 in) pieces. *Cansalada viada,* which more or less means "streaky" *cansalada,* is a cured but unsmoked pork belly bacon. As bacon can mean a few things in English-speaking countries, going with a fatty pancetta is probably your best bet. And to be honest, using a great artisanal smoked bacon might not be authentic but it will undoubtedly taste great. Whatever you use, it should be fatty… this is not the time to think lean and green.

3 cloves of garlic sliced thinly, lengthwise
salt to taste

Traditionally and understandably, a shepherd in the high mountains of the Cerdanya would use but one pot to cook both the potatoes and the cabbage, adding the cabbage at just the right moment to the already cooking potatoes. I use this technique but honestly it's easier and more precise to cook the cabbage and potatoes in separate cooking vessels.

1   In one large pot add the potatoes and cover with water. Bring to a boil, add about a teaspoon of salt, cook until fork tender, then drain, leaving the potatoes in the pot.

2   In the other pot add water and bring to a boil. Add another teaspoon of salt and then the cabbage. Cook until tender and then drain.

3   While the potatoes and cabbage are still cooking, take a skillet, and without adding any oil to the pan, fry the *cansalada*-like pork product, erring on the crispy side. Remove the *cansalada*, lower the heat and fry the garlic until it is just golden. Add a little olive oil to the pan if your *cansalada*/bacon was too lean and you couldn't render out some fat. You want an ample amount of "drippin's." Don't burn the garlic. I repeat do not burn the garlic. Remove the garlic, reserve the now garlic-flavored rendered fat.

4   Add the cabbage to the potatoes and, with a sturdy fork, mash until everything is more or less well-combined. You don't want to end up with a gooey vegetable and starch paste. Go easy on the mashing so that the ingredients are still discernable. You can add salt at this point but remember that there will potentially be lots of this from both the *cansalada* and the rendered fat. Once combined, the *trinxat* can be served mashed potato style and dressed with the *cansalada*, the fried garlic slivers, and a dribble of the rendered fat. Pinotxo uses a ring mold and so can you. Pile in the *trinxat*, remove the mold and top with the aforementioned goodies. You can if you wish add a dollop of olive oil.

FIDEUÀ

ROSSEJAT

As mentioned elsewhere, a *paella magnifica* is a difficult dish to conjure. But at least in my *casa*, it's *Fideuà*, not *paella*, that gets the warmer welcome. "**SO WHAT'S A FIDEUÀ?**" Simply put it's a dish of short stubby *pasta* called *fideos*. And like a *paella*, it too comes from the Valencia region. While it's often referred to as "**A NOODLE PA-ELLA**" I don't think that aptly describes what, to my mind, is one of the world's great *pasta* dishes. And as you might suspect, as Spain is a nation of pueblitos (little villages), there is no shortage of variations nor origin stories which usually feature a fishing boat, missing ingredients, a hungry captain and a crafty cook. And like rice dishes, you have dry types, wet types, in-between types, seafood versions, landfood versions, and *mar i muntanya* versions. Some are are cooked in a *paella* (remember in "**VALENCIANO**" the word for the pan is the same as for the dish... *paella*...), and others that are cooked in a *cazuela*. Still, it breaks down to two main types: "**FIDEUÀ**" and "**FIDEUÀ ROSSEJAT**". Not to oversimplify, but the difference is basically this: to toast the noodles (meaning to "**ROSSEJAR**", "**BLOND-IFY**"... or "**TO MAKE GOLDEN**"), or not to bother.

So let's "bother" and make the toasted version. As is the case with rice dishes, the success of this dish is dependent on two things: the ratio of the liquid to the pasta and the quality of that liquid. As said throughout this book, it's all in the *"caldo."*

Paella pans are dirt cheap, particularly if you buy the right one, and the right one is black and enameled. They are relatively easy to clean, don't warp too much and they look great on the table. This recipe serves 4 people and will require a 40 centimeter pan. Yes, it's possible to slide the number of diners to size of pan ratio around a little bit but if you are going to have 12 people over you should probably buy a 60 centimeter *paella*. But then the question is how do you heat up such a monster? Which brings us back to bonfires and guys named Juanjo and burning tar paper. Are you going to feed 8 to 10? Buy two 40 centimeter pans and double the recipe or add another dish. Why all the fussing about pan size? It's like this. Both the rice in a *paella* and the *fideos* in a *fideuà* are supposed to be cooked in a thin layer. This is what makes these dishes controllable, predictable, and ultimately delicious. If you vary the pan size too much you'll end up with your rice or pasta being either overcooked or undercooked. What you want is *al dente*... not too soft but definitely not "crunchy."

400 g (14 oz) # 2 fideos (See "Provisions", page 67)

1 l (4 cups) of chicken stock, heated. Some might say that a fideua cannot be made with anything other than fish stock. They might say it, but they would be wrong. (See "It's the *Caldo*...", page 136)

So, to break this down, 1 pretty hefty serving equals 100 grams (3.5 oz) of pasta to 250 ml (1 cup) of stock. Got 6 people? Slide the numbers around but take a gander at the information about pan size to the right. Remember, in Spain an assortment of smaller dishes is preferable to one large portion. Feel free to down scale.

1 medium onion, chopped thinly

2 cloves of garlic, minced

2 medium tomatoes, grated (See "*El secret del tomàquet beneïda*", page 76)

extra virgin olive oil

salt to taste

1. Preheat oven to 220º C/425º F.
2. Heat up the *paella* to medium and add a hearty pour of olive oil.
3. Swish the oil around the pan to evenly coat the bottom and lower the heat to medium low.
4. Add the garlic and saute until golden and then remove and reserve.
5. Add the *fideos* and, using a spatula, spread them evenly around the pan and *rossejar* (toast) them. Let's be honest. This part is less than scientific. There will be some pasta that gets a little too dark and some bit under toasted. All is good... just don't burn them. We are not making blackened spaghetti. Once the *fideos* are *rossejat*, slide them out of the pan and reserve.

6. As you have learned from just about every recipe in this book you will now make a *sofregit*. Lower the heat, add another splash of olive oil, and gently saute the onions until they are golden and nearly jam like. Add the grated tomatoes and the previously toasted garlic and cook for a few more minutes. Spread the *sofregit* evenly around the pan.
7. Return the *fideos* to the pan and distribute them evenly.
8. Sprinkle about one half teaspoon of salt over the pasta, add the stock, then increase the temperature to high, and bring to a boil.
9. Reduce to medium, and after 3 minutes or so reduce the heat to a slightly aggressive simmer. When the *fideos* have absorbed most of the liquid (this should take around 20 minutes but the only real way to know if they are done is to taste test them for doneness and by taking a peek to see if there is any extra liquid bubbling away... if so continue until it's mostly absorbed).
10. Transfer the paella to the oven. At some point much of the pasta should "stand up" or as they say here, "*erectos como el órgano sexual masculino.*" I will let you translate this one. This last part of the operation should take 5 minutes or less. Let your eyes be your guide. Take a look at the photo on page 134.
11. You can also engorge your pasta by covering the pan with any sports section from Barcelona's daily newspaper, La Vanguardia, that features at least one photo of football superstar Lionel Messi. OK, don't worry about obtaining a copy of the sports section (any old newspaper will do) but do worry about your noodle cover bursting into flames. Again 5 minutes should engorge the pasta nicely.
13. The traditional way of eating this is to first taste, comment positively on the delicate flavor and then drown the dish in *all i oli* (the recipe for which you can find on page 84).

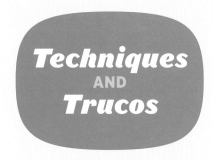

Techniques AND **Trucos**

IT'S THE CALDO...

Goodness in, goodness out. Simply great stuff made simply with lots of love and care. These are the ingredients of the secret sauce of the cuina de Pinotxo.

Since we have established that braising is one of the dominant techniques in the small but mighty Pinotxo kitchen, the importance of the braising liquid can not be taken lightly. It's the *caldo*... it's the broth... it's the stock.

So how does one get a great stock? Here in Spain I can just go to the mercado or to my butcher and buy it. Can you do this where you live? Not to worry, with very little trouble you can make your own.

The premise is simple. Simmer boney meat for a long time. Let's use a *caldo de pollo* (chicken stock) as our model.

Again I am at a slight advantage as I can just go buy chicken carcasses at any of the above places. They cost hardly anything and they have so much flavor. You, on the other hand...well again, not to worry. Get to the closest butcher and ask nicely. All those boneless, skinless chicken breasts at some point were attached to a... chicken. So I would think that there is a good chance that the part that they were attached to (the carcass) might just be waiting for you. Good luck in your quest.

Now once you have acquired our meatless chicken here's what to do.

Take a large lidded pot and add our usual hearty pour of olive oil then over medium heat lightly "brown" the carcasses. The carcasses are not exactly regularly shaped nor are they compact, so you are probably going to have to brown them individually. You just want to sear the bones and the remaining meat. There is a scientific principle behind this but in the interest of moving along let's just ignore it… simply put… its just makes the *caldo* taste better.

Remove the carcasses, lower the heat, and add a bit more olive oil to the pot. "*Sofregir*" the onions. When they are golden add the carcasses, the cloves of garlic, then add water to cover everything. Bring to a boil and then reduce to a simmer. Cover the pot and let it percolate at a very low simmer for at least a couple of hours. Once you have completed this part of the operation remove the carcasses and discard. Strain the liquid through a sieve. Return the liquid to the pot and again bring to a boil. Leaving the pot uncovered, reduce the liquid by 30 to 50 percent. Salt to taste. Bravo. You have just made a great *caldo* which can be used anytime one is called for in this book or the world beyond. And Señor or Señora "*Caldero/a*", you can do the same thing with meaty beef and or veal bones.

Ingredients:
a couple chicken carcasses
water
6 or so cloves of garlic, peeled and halved lengthwise
3 onions, chopped coarsely
extra virgin olive oil
salt

ARROZ CALDOSO *con* POLLO *y* SETAS

PAELLA, PAELLA, PAELLA... I'm going to go out on a limb here and risk the wrath of thousands of bars, restaurants, and roadside quicky stops. There's lots and lots of *paella* in España, the vast majority of which is, at best, mediocre. Why? I think some of it is our own fault, and by our I mean we *turistas*. We expats. We estranjeros. Most *paella* is made the way we expect it to be made... like a Disney cartoon. In the Delta de Ebro (which is arguably Spain's most important rice growing area and is 160 km south of Barcelona) *paella* was, and still is, very much another one of those dishes designed to *aprovechar*... to take advantage of what's on hand. And what's on hand is, obviously, rice and bits of whatever. Rabbit, chicken, snails, maybe some fava beans, and if it's your birthday, one lonely local *gamba*. It's not something out of **"FERDINAND THE BULL"**... piled high with clams, mussels, strips of bright red bell peppers, peas, *chorizo*, ham, mussels, clams, and giant irradiated **"TIGER PRAWNS**™**"** from an Asian shrimp farm, all riding on a sea of screamin' yellow rice. Hey, why not just toss in some Manchengo cheese and *pepitas de chocolate* while you are at it. *Olé!*

The other thing about *paella*, even for Iberians, is that it's a dish rife with familial voodoo; ghosts of long lost relatives, tipsy uncles, and testosterone engorged padrinos, all fighting for *machista* turf during one of the few times that the men folk actually do something culinary. **"JUANJO! HURRAY! FETCH THAT BIG ROCK NEXT TO THE TAR PAPER, THE PAELLA IS LEANING! DON'T GET THE FIRE TOO CLOSE TO THE GAS TANK! OK, WHO HAS THE SPORTS SECTION? REMEMBER MESSI'S FACE MUST BE PLACED FACE DOWN ON THE RICE. WHAT DO YOU MEAN WE ONLY HAVE EL PAÍS! JODER TÍO! MARIA! BRING ME A BEER!"**

And there are other vague notions like **"THE SOCARRAT"** which is reputed to be the crunchy bit just toasted on the bottom of the pan. I have rarely seen a **"SOCARRAT"** but I have eaten quite a lot of burnt rice. Truthfully, it's not that difficult of a dish to do well, as the few establishments that turn-out a great version demonstrate. What do they have that you probably don't have? A really big oven... where they wisely finish the dish at a very specific temperature for a very specific amount of time. Like Uncle Ben's… it's perfect every time.

As we know, Pinotxo is a tiny bar and has no room for giant ovens or racks of *paella* pans (actually paella means pan so it's little redundant). What they do make "**ON OCCASION**" and "**TO ORDER**" is an *Arroz Caldoso*, AKA Soupy Rice. It is absolutely delicious, fairly easy to make, and you don't need Lionel Messi lying face down in your dinner. So, before we get started, let us discuss the notion of "**SOUPY**".

In many real deal rice houses there will, on occasion, be three distinct levels of liquidity. There is the previously discussed "**PAELLA**", which should be dry and cooked in a thin band in the aforementioned wide, shallow pan. There is *"Arroz Meloso"* (which does not mean damp… but sweet and mellow… but to my *guiri* ears sounds like something you have removed by a dermatologist) and then there is *"Arroz Caldoso."* So *paella* translates to dry, *meloso* means slightly soupier (risotto-like), and finally there is *caldoso*, which means you are having soup… with rice. So technically we are making an *"Arroz Meloso"* but we are still going to call it *"Arroz Caldoso"* because that's what everybody calls it even though it's not.

SERVES 4 AS AN ENTREE

2	chicken thigh/leg combos, cut up as for a *paella* (into 3 or 4 pieces)
2	medium onions, finely chopped
200 g	(½ lb) wild mushrooms (chanterelles, etc.), chopped into bite-size chunks
500 g	(1 lb) of a good bomba rice
1.5 l	(6.5 cups) of a great *caldo de pollo* (See "It's the Caldo", page 136)
100 ml	(4 oz) dry white wine
	A pinch of saffron, crumbled
	A small palmful of dried or fresh rosemary, chopped or crumbled
	extra virgin olive oil
	Salt to taste

1   Add a hearty splash of olive oil to a *cazuela* or deep pot and fry the chicken over medium heat until golden brown. Remove.

2   Adding a bit more olive oil, make a *sofregit* (See "Sofregit", page 78) of the onions.

3   Add mushrooms, saffron, and rosemary. When the mushrooms are slightly browned add the white wine. Let the wine reduce for a few minutes.

4   Add the rice and return the chicken to the *cazuela*.

5   Add the *caldo* and reduce the heat to low.

6   The rice should be finished in approximately 15 minutes. Test the rice for doneness… I like mine a little bit al dente… with a slight bite in the center of the rice… risotto style. Some of my "citified" Spanish/Catalan friends prefer it to be pretty much cooked all the way through.

RABO *de* TORO

As Caterina and her father walked from Andalusia to Barcelona, so this dish makes a journey of its own, by way of the **CORRIDA DE TOROS**, from Cordoba to Catalunya, with a little help from Islam.

Rabo means tail and *toro* means bull, and considering Spain's long and bloody history with the *toreo*, and their propensity for letting nothing go to waste, is it any wonder that this dish exists?

In Catalunya the *corrida* is now officially verboten and bulls can pursue other career opportunities–like eating grass and having sex with cows. Thankfully, this makes real bull tails harder to come by. Still, one can make a very respectable *rabo de toro* with a *rabo de buey*… cow.

The Pinotxo *equipo* are pretty much firmly split down the middle regarding their favorite dishes… there is the *cap-i-pota* crowd and there is the faccion de *rabo de toro*. Me, I'm a *rabo* fan. Bone meat dishes like this, *galtes* (pig or veal cheeks… I like *cerdo*) and *espalda de cordero* (lamb shoulder) are for me the most indulgently carnivorous of all the cuts of animalia. It's that fabulously flavorful intersection of meat and *hueso* (bone) and all the parts that connect the two. Hey, it's not like a hamburger, where you are spared the notion that you are indeed consuming another life form. When you're digging into a plate of *rabo* there is no doubt that what you're eating was not too long ago swatting away flies. Maybe it even had a name. For me, understanding and respecting this is part of the bargain of being a carnivore.

There are lot's of recipes for *rabo*, but Jordi's version differs in the use of the verb *reposar*, to rest. This version takes three days to make with generous pauses between stages. To deviate will not ruin your life or your *rabo*, but then you won't be serving the dish that causes the aficionados to line up six deep on Saturday mornings.

RE
CI
PE

750 g (1.5 lb) to 1 kg (2 lb) *rabo de toro* (OK, it's called oxtail)

Hopefully, your butcher will be skilled in cutting the rabo into the appropriate 7.5 cm (3 in) chunks. And since you have been able to find a butcher that can find a rabo, he or she will more than likely be able to deliver the goods.

2 leeks, chopped into 1.5 cm (1/2 in) disks

3 ripe medium tomatoes, grated using the Catalan grating trick (See "*El secret del tomàquet beneït*", page 76)

2 red peppers, seeded and cut into eighths

4 cloves of garlic, minced

4 carrots, peeled and sliced into 1.5 cm (1/2 in) disks

12 whole peppercorns

A pre-made bouquet garni or a couple of bay leaves and 1 branch each of dried rosemary and oregano

A strong Rioja like red wine

2 teaspoons *Pimentón de la vera, dulce*

flour

extra virgin olive oil

fresh ground pepper

salt

DAY 1

1 Sprinkle a little salt on both sides of the *rabo* and dust with flour.
2 Add the olive oil to a *cazuela*, a deep pot or a dutch oven, that has been preheated to medium heat.
3 Brown the *rabo* on all sides and remove.
4 Keeping the *suc* (juice) that has perhaps exited the rabo in the same pot, make a *sofregit* (yes... it's true) of the leeks. (See *Sofregit*, page 78) Once they take on a little color, add successively the garlic, the peppers, the carrots, and the tomatoes.
5 Once everything is nice, soft, and delicious looking, remove from the heat and return the meat. After it's cooled down a bit, *reposar* phase one in the refrigerator for twenty-four hours.

DAY 2

6 Remove the *rabo* and *sofregit* mixture from the refrigerator and let return to room temperature.
7 Add enough wine to nearly submerge the ingredients.
8 Bring to a boil and lower to a slow simmer. Cover and continue to simmer for at least 2 hours or until the meat is "fallin' off the bone" tender.
9 Let it cool and then return to the refrigerator for another twenty-four hours.

DAY 3

10 Return to room temperature and sprinkle in the *pimentón*.
11 If the cooking liquids have been absorbed or evaporated by the previous day's simmering, add a little water to make a thick-ish *salsa*. If perchance they have not been absorbed or evaporated, reduce the liquids over a very low heat until the *salsa* has thickened to your liking. Warm up to serving temperature, plate the chow, and look for a location to open up a restaurant. You may now say, "*Ole!*"
12 Serve with rice or for the full taverna de Cordoba experience, *patatas fritas* (*papas fritas* in Andaluz or... French fries).

GO SOAK YOUR BEANS

Canned goods (See *El Rebost*, page 102), preserved meats and fish, and legumes (beans, rice, pulses) are a large part of Spanish cooking due to España's Franco era shaky electrical system and the resultant lack of refrigeration. This called for the ability to time-shift the harvest without the benefit of a dependable electrical grid. Franco, who had a tiny, squeaky voice and undoubtedly a very small…(I'm sorry, I will stop there), also did things like change the gauge of the railways so that they wouldn't hook up with the rest of the world. Don't you just love a dictator?

As one would think, at a place with as much history as Pinotxo, these ingredients make a regular appearance on the menu.

Again, living in Spain, it's very easy for me to drop by the *mercado* and hit a *parada* for a whack of *legumbres* that are pre-soaked and ready to use. There are tubs brimming with lentils, *garbanzos*, and every kind of bean you can imagine. I used to buy the dried ones, but to be honest, the ready to use ones are just as good and usually about the same price. You, however, probably don't have this luxury, so here's how the soaking/cooking thing works.

RULE 1: Lentils do not have to be soaked. You can just put them in a pot, cover them with an inch of stock or water, and cook over a low heat until tender.

RULE 2: Cooking times are not applicable. Every bean is different. Cook them until they are done.

That said, here's the official, certified *Abuela* technique for soaking your bean or beans, as the case may be.

Put your legume of choice in some sort of container… like for example a bowl. Cover them with an inch or so of room-temperature water. As the beans "drink" the water, continue to top them off. I usually put them on the coffee table and periodically add water while I watch reruns of Zorro. For some reason this seems to make them tastier. This dance takes about eight hours so if you need to get some shut eye, add enough water so that the beans can drink overnight. Go right ahead… better to drown them than to find dry, thirsty, and bad tempered beans when you wake up in the morning. Now drain your beans… why? I'll just say that if you don't, your meal can get a little noisy. OK, that covers bean soaking. So how do you cook them?

If you have a pressure cooker you can save a lot of time. I don't and, to be honest, they scare me so I really can't tell you much about that process. I, however, have a number of pots (some even have lids). So what I do is put the beans or the lentils in said pot and again cover them with one inch of water. Bring to a boil. Reduce to a simmer and let them cook until they are tender. Don't talk yourself into some nonsense about *Fesols de Santa Pau al dente*… there is no culture in the world that likes beans with a crunchy, raw center. The beans will be done when they are done… and this can be anywhere from a half an hour to half a day. *Garbanzos* and black beans tend to really take their own sweet time. Oh well, you can always keep yourself busy by making a whack of *sofregit* or *samfaina,* or watching more Zorro reruns. And yes, I am fully aware that Zorro was set in Colonial California but he was played by Antonio Banderas in the 1993 remake, and Antonio Banderas worked with Pedro Almodovar, so there.

What can you do to jazz them up? Salt is always a good addition, as are aromatics like bay leaf and thyme, as is cooking the lentils in a meat or vegetable stock. Note to Americans… One word: Bacon. Feel free to fry some up and add it. Generally speaking, I prefer my legumes au-naturel, with little to no spices, just as God intended, and let the other ingredients carry the day.

Regarding those potential unpleasant noises… add a teaspoon of baking soda whilst they are cooking. It seems to actually work.

When I was a kid, we heard a troubling rumor that crazy Italians actually ate mussels... you know those black things that clung to the sides of the pilings at the boat dock. We used to use crack them open and use them for bait. It was unthinkable that anyone could possibly choke down these weird, alien, orange polyps. We also thought corn dogs were exotic fare, and that a lime jello mold embedded with fruit cocktail and topped off with a dollop of "**SALAD DRESSING**" was about as good as it got. I, like most baby boomers, led a very sheltered childhood culinary-wise. I'm not dissing corn dogs or things suspended in lime jello but at some point my taste buds were introduced to a more diverse and adventurous world of flavors and I have never looked back. OK, there was that one time with the Saharawi refugees and the camel hump... but I'll save that story for after we have eaten.

Mussels, *mejillones*, moules, and cozze, are served, one way or another, in just about every restaurant located within a hundred miles of any salt water in Europe. Again, what separates Pinotxo from the herd is the quality of the ingredients and the simplicity of the preparation.

MUSCLOS AMB ÇEBA I TOMÀQUET

1 kg	(2 lb) high quality mussels, cleaned
3	medium onions, chopped coarsely
3	medium grated, ripe tomatoes (See *"El secret del tomàquet beneïda"*, page 76)
1	lemon, quartered
	whole peppercorns
	a few dried bay leaves
250 ml	(8 oz) of dry white wine
	extra virgin olive oil

1. Place the mussels, the white wine, and the lemon in a large pot. Cover the pot and increase the heat to high (a glass pot lid helps in this pursuit, if not check regularly... be careful of the steam). As soon as the mussels open, immediately remove them from the heat. Again, like the *Remenat de Tallerinas* (page 110), the idea is capture as much of the mussel's liquid as possible.
2. Strain the liquid through a super fine strainer, a cloth colander or cheesecloth and reserve.
3. In another pot or *cazuela,* add a hearty pour of olive oil and make a sofregit by slowly cooking the onions until they are soft and translucent.
4. Add the bay leaves, pepper, and the grated tomatoes. Over a low flame, stir until the tomatoes are cooked.
5. Add the mussels and the reserved juice, give it a stir, and then cover. Simmer over low heat until everything is warmed through. Serve with the sofregit scattered about the mussels.

ESCALIVADA

Like many other things in our book, *Escalivada* is a visit to a simpler time, a time before *sous vide, espuma,* and spherification… an earthy return to when our ancestors threw raw ingredients into a fire and then, at great peril, fished out the results.

Of all the recipes in the book, this may be the one that you make every week… and why not? It tastes amazing, could not be more healthy, and the technique used, as mentioned above, could not be more simple.

OK WHAT EXACTLY IS ESCALIVADA…? WELL, IT'S ANOTHER ONE OF THOSE DISHES BASED ON A VERB. TO "ESCALIVAR" MEANS TO COOK IN ASHES. SEE I TOLD YOU… "TOSS INTO THE FIRE AND…"

Traditionally, the dish is made by placing whole red bell peppers, unpeeled onions, and eggplants, on either a grill or directly on the red hot embers of a fire until they are "**COOKED**." Once you have decided they are done, you remove and toss the skins and peels (which have protected the edible parts of the vegetables from the unpleasantly inedible crunchy coals and ashes) and… that's it. Maybe add little olive oil, maybe a little salt but nada mas.

Listen, if you have a barbeque or an open fire, and you are feeling suitably caveman or cave woman like by all means, give this traditional version a shot but if you are looking for a consistent and convenient way to make this dish, do what most Catalans do. Put the whole magilla in the *horno*, close the door and call it a day. Yes, you will miss the elemental karma of smoke, char, and potential third degree burns, but you will exchange these for something that you will actually want to do on a regular basis.

2 or 3   large red bell peppers
2 or 3   medium onions (peeled)
2   medium eggplants that are on the long
        and skinny side

1 Preheat oven to 175º C/350º F.

2 Place vegetables on an oven tray or in a hotel pan (you know one of those rectangular stainless steel numbers) or on a deeply lipped cookie sheet. Be forewarned, liquids will exit the cooking vegetables. The more you protect your cookware, the less you will have to clean up later. Personally, I use one of those silicone oven mats. They work great.

3 Place tray on the middle rack of the oven. If you have a convection setting use it. If not, don't worry.

4 Leave it be for 45 minutes or so. If the peppers are getting a little black, flip them. While you are at it, do the same to the onions and the eggplants.

5 Continue cooking until everything is very soft and liquid is issuing forth from the onions and peppers. Try to save this juice.

6 Remove from the oven and allow to cool. Or go for the authentic experience of trying to peel incendiary onions with your bare hands. If you are following the former technique, don't wait too long, as it's easier to skin the vegetables while they are on the warm side.

TO PEEL:

PEPPERS

- Cut off the top of the peppers and take out the seeds. Cut the peppers in half and remove the now "plasticy" peel. Cut into coarse strips.

ONIONS

- Cut a bit off the top and the bottoms of the onions. Slide off the inedible layers. Cut in two, lengthwise.

EGGPLANT

- Cut the top off. Cut in two, lengthwise. Remove the flesh with a spoon and, with your hands, separate the pulp into strips. Serve with olive oil and coarse salt. If you are wise you will take the juice you rescued from the oven tray (you did save the juice, didn't you?) and apply it generously.

Techniques AND Trucos

Braise moi

"La bonne cuisine est la base du véritable bonheur."
Auguste Escoffier

OK... I hate it when folks drop a line in French without a translation into an everyday, slangy conversation, particularly when it comes from a guy named Auguste Escoffier. "Dude! La bonne cuisine est la véritable bonheur!" But it is a great quote and translates to, "Good food is the foundation of real happiness." I completely agree. Here's another from the great cook and culinary sage: "The greatest dishes are the simplest dishes." Yes, you betcha, and braising, one of Auguste's favorite techniques, is one of the simplest, greatest, and most rewarding things you can do in your designated cooking space. Think about your Grandma's pot roast, a North African tagine, collard greens and potlikker, schweinebraten, Vietnamese Bò kho, and Asian hot pots. All are so easy, and any of them can drop people to their knees with just plain tastiness.

Following the master's mandate, cooking at Pinotxo is a simple affair that, with the exception of rice dishes, and the steamed mussels, mostly breaks down into three basic techniques; braising, sauteing and grilling.

So what is this braising you speak of? Well, in France, a braisier is a sort of lowish, thick-walled cast iron covered pot. It's a relative of that Dutch oven you might have picked up at a garage sale. In España it's pretty much our old friend, the remarkable clay cazuela (See "What's in a Pot", page 107) that comes in a number of dimensions. So *braisier...* a heavy duty pot with a tight fitting lid, "braising" what you do in said cooking vessel. Please do not confuse this with *baise...* which is another French word and is unsuitable for a family publication.

Braising is basically this: something (meat, poultry, vegetables, and sometimes fish) is seared over high heat. Then a liquid (stock, wine, beer, brandy, water, etc.) is added to a level that is between one-quarter and three-quarters of the depth of the ingredients. The liquid is brought to a boil and then immediately reduced to an almost imperceptible "simmer", (they use the absolutely wonderful phrase *"xup, xup"* in Catalunya). The pot is covered, and you then go about your business for, say, anywhere from one hour to several days. Meat-wise, the process converts the fattier, cologenier, bonier, "cheaper" cuts into something that makes anyone who ordered a porterhouse wish they had erred on the frugal side. Use this information as you will, but remember, with great knowledge comes great responsibility, so don't be surprised if you suddenly become incredibly popular. Oh... can you use that crock pot stuck back behind the VHS tapes and orphaned socks? Oh my... yes. Drag it out.

S ometimes special things happen. Sometimes it all works out. Sometimes someone breaks an egg just for you.

One fine Saturday morning I dropped by Pinotxo right in the middle of one of their many rushes. There is the six-thirty a.m. morning rush where every fruit, oyster, or offal seller hits the bar for one of their famous en vidrio three decker *cafés con leche*. There is the *esmorzar de forquilla* rush... the beer and *bocadillo* break, (better known in the US as the coffee break), where a varied selection of office workers, newspaper, flower, and reptile vendors from las Ramblas, along with an audience of puzzled tourists wondering why shapely calved, high heeled wearing secretaries are eating squid, and drinking Pilsner Urquell at ten in the morning. Then there is the inevitable twelve o'clock "**WELL DAMN IT JUNE, THIS IS WHEN WE EAT IN FORT WAYNE SO THIS IS WHEN WE EAT HERE, AND WHAT THE HECK IS CAP-I-POTA 'SPOSED TO BE?**" rush. Then the six deep at the bar, all hell breaking out "hey buster, could you eat your garbanzos and morilla a little faster?" lunch rush which lasts anywhere from one o'clock to four o'clock.

I hit rush number two and it's Saturday, so you have to add in the, "Let's go shopping but first a vermut and some clams" contingent. Be sure to multiply everything by a factor of four because it's, well, like I said, Saturday. So Jordi gives me that look indicating that my time has come to order, and I had better make it quick. I go for a *truita de bacalla*, which we have learned is not a trout but a delicate, individual sized tortilla with salt cod. Head shake... nope, all out. Try again. Before I can say "Botifarra" Jordi says, "You want an egg?" Sure, I'll have an egg. The place is nuts. Just let em off the hook. Just take the easy path.

I also order a "cañita" (a small beer... or a big beer depending on who's pouring), made time with a personalized USB stick salesman from Shenzhen, "Anything, any shape you want... Scooby Doo, LeBron James, Barack Obama...", and a local regular who told me all about all of the pig parts that could be considered bacon.

JORDI'S SATURDAY MORNING EGG

Jordi returns with a plate layered from bottom to top with thin slices of crispy fried, hand cut potatoes, *pancetta* (I got a thumbs up from the regular), and one perfectly fried egg on top. By perfect I mean slightly crispy around the edge, a not under nor over cooked white, and a yolk that's ever so slightly opaque. A touch of sea salt, pan con tomate on the side, and another cañita to wash it all down.

You know, writing this gives me an unquenchable desire to hop on my bike and head down to the Boqueria. I guess that says it all.

1 perfect egg from a happy chicken

1 slice of thinly sliced pancetta (Ok... use thinly sliced bacon if you have to... it will still taste great)

A few thin but irregularly cut slices of potato (Like maybe 6, peeled or unpeeled...I shall leave it up to you and your sense of patience)

extra virgin olive oil

flakey sea salt

freshly ground black pepper or *Pimentón de la Vera*, *picante* or *dulce*

1 Place a squirt of olive in a small skillet... or any skillet that you may have. Again, a quality non-stick pan will save your life.

2 Add the pancetta to the pan. Cook until done but not too crispy. Remove.

3 Add potatoes to pan.

4 Over medium heat, fry until done. Contrary to popular belief, using a lower temperature to fry things like potatoes is perfectly OK... unlike higher temperatures, you end up with potatoes that are not burnt on the outside and raw in the middle. Cook until "fork tender." Remove.

5 Break the egg or eggs, as the case may be, directly into the pan.

6 When the white is neither runny nor transparent, and the yolk has just gone ever so slightly "opaque", you are done. You may also cover said pan for a little more doneness.... but you do want the yolks to be "runny." Alternatively, those with a steady wrist and aim may gently flip the egg and do without the lid.

7 Plate the potatoes and the pancetta and then top with the fried egg.

8 Add a sprinkle of sea salt and maybe a slight dusting of *Pimentón de la vera* or fresh ground black pepper, y esta.

9 This is an example or variation on the lovely dish, *Huevos Estrellados*... which can, depending on who you are talking to, mean eggs sunny side up, just a fried egg or eggs over easy. Generally it means a fried egg on top of something else... that something else usually being potatoes.

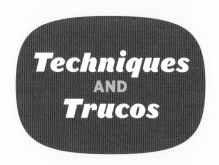

A LA PLANCHA: *Utensilio, generalmente electrodoméstico, que sirve para planchar. Placa de metal sobre la que se asan o cocinan alimentos: pescado a la plancha.*

In Spanish a plancha is many things: a clothes iron, a flat-top metal surface for grilling, and a cooking technique. Can you use a clothes iron to "planchar" shrimp? I suppose so, and if you hit the crustaceans with the turbo steam button you might just invent a new culinary methodology. Remember, the whole *espuma* thing was started when someone gave Ferran Adrià an aerosol whip cream gadget. He promptly threw away the warranty, stuffed in an oyster and gained another Michelin star.

So then, one of Pinotxo's most popular dishes is *Gambas a la plancha*. Does this mean that Juanito fires up the Rowenta and presses your crustacean? No, one of the boys tosses some hand picked, and very recently kicking, gambas on the flat top, sprinkles on a little salt, flips them once, slips them on a plate and that's it. Within seconds you are tearing off the shells and plucking off their tiny little legs with your bare hands. If you're wise, you are also ripping off the head and removing the brains with one hearty suck. This is what a la plancha is all about. Perfect ingredients plus searing heat, steam, sounds, smells, and sizzles equals lunch.

Can you do this at home? Of course you can. Do you need a commercial griddle? No. You just need a very hot pan and some terrific raw ingredients. Shrimp, meat, a butterflied chicken breast, vegetables. *Vamos!*

Next up is a complete step by step exploration of *"Gambas a la plancha"*... wait a minute... there is really only one step. Take food... cook food. Oh... one more. Eat food.

GAMBAS
a la plancha

Let this be a lesson to you. You can, if you are pure of heart, intent, and resolute to the core, build an empire on the simplest of things. In this case, shrimp, or as some of my friends from New Jersey say, shrimps.

But this brings up another question of taxonomy. What is a prawn and what is a shrimp? The Food and Agriculture Organization of the United Nations (FAO) say that both shrimp and prawns are a decapod crustacean of the suborder natantia (don't you just love wikipedia?). Specifically, the scientific name for this animal is Dendrobranchiata... wait, wait, wait... what's this about... hold on... Caridea... isn't that one of those diseases you get from... no, that's another shrimp/prawn thing which has a different gill structure and a second abdominal segment. Hmmm... why don't we just give up and let our pals from Jersey guide us... "**DEES TINGS ARE ALL SHRIMPS, YOUSE GOT YOUR BIG SHRIMPS AND YOUSE GOT YOUR SMALL SHRIMPS.**" But what kind do they have at Pinotxo? They have big red shrimps... known 'round these parts as "**GAMBAS DE PALAMÓS**" and scientifically as "**ARISTEUS ANTENNATUS.**"

PALAMÓS IS A PLEASANT TOWN ABOUT 120 KILOMETERS FROM BARCELONA WHERE MY PAL JORDI GALIN HAS A NICE LITTLE WEEKEND GETAWAY. IT IS ALSO WHERE TRUMAN CAPOTE WROTE MUCH OF "IN COLD BLOOD" AND UNDOUBTEDLY COMPLAINED BITTERLY ABOUT THE THREAD COUNT OF THE BED LINENS. "DO ALL DOSE RED SHRIMPS COME FROM PALAMÓS?" No, they also come from a few towns on the Costa Brava, like Roses, Blanes and l'Escala. Anyway, they are very red, very tasty, and damn expensive due to the fact that every once in a while they disappear altogether. They are also never, ever, ever frozen. But look, with most fish and some *mariscos* (like shrimp), in these days of modern, at sea freezing technology, it's not a terrible thing to do. However, let me tell you, fresh, right off the boat beauties like these are really a different breed of decapod.

So what can you do, in say, Cherokee, Iowa? You are going to look for the best, big, whole, unpeeled, head and everything, shrimps you can find. They may very well come from Argentina or Chile, and in your case this is OK... because let's face it, your mile 0 decapod options are going to be a crawdad or Mrs. Paul's. If you happen to live in a coastal area, acquire some of these animals at a high-end yuppie fish joint or any decent, decidedly non-yuppie Chinatown market. Anyway, buy some nice big shrimps. And if you must, thaw them out slowly in the refrigerator. Now that your shrimps dilemma has been solved, read on.

2 to 6 large shrimps (heads on, foots on, shells on... everything on) per person

small squirt of good olive oil

really lovely, flakey sea salt

1 Put oil in pan.
2 Heat pan.
3 Put shrimps in pan.
4 Sprinkle shrimps with salt.
5 When one side is all pink and done looking turn the shrimps.
6 Sprinkle salt on other side.
7 When the other side is all pink and done looking remove from pan and put on plate.
8 Remember, unlike brownies, a fish is done when it turns opaque. And since these shrimps have their shells on, it's a little hard to tell. When in doubt, it's best to err on the undercooked side.

Eating instructions:
1 Snap off head.
2 Suck out stuff in head.

Option A: Remove shell.
1 Eat Shrimp.

Option B: Don't remove shell.
1 Eat Shrimp and shell like me and 1.3 billion Chinese people do (it's good for your articulations).
2 Save tails for handicraft projects.

IBERIAN EATING

There is something in the dirt. Something old. Something that is both light and dark. Something deep, profound, animal, and spiritual. I see it, feel it, smell it everyday when I do something as mundane as getting a cup of coffee. To the sound of two cycle engines and chattering throngs, I look up and see the sky and how the orange light is falling on the mishmash of buildings; and then down at the street. And I know there is something beneath it all.

Spain is tied to the primordial, to the neolithic, a past well before civilization, architecture and the Phoenicians, Greeks and Romans. You can see it in how the people here deal with life. The bonfires in the city streets on the night of San Juan... to make it through the night, to see the sun, the sadness and darkness of winter, the patterns and rhythms of their days, weeks, seasons, years, lives. Yes, they have big screens, BMWs, purported twenty-five percent unemployment, a government, that, up to the recent elections, seemed to function solely on graft and cronyism; yet magic is still part of a regular breakfast here.

The people here are not fond of radical change. They thrive on the predictable. They want the markets to reflect what's in the trees and the fields. They like the food that their grandmothers made for them. *Croquetas*, *estofadas*, *albóndigas*, *arroz caldoso*, *cocido*. It's like the heart of this cooking, *samfaina*; at its most basic it's only olive oil, tomatoes, onions, and a little bit of garlic cooked for what seems like an eternity. Oil first, then onions, then the garlic, then the tomatoes and a pinch of salt. Stir lightly, slowly, for as long as you can while meditating on whether or not the fish lady slipped you "previously" frozen *cigales*, on Messi's heroic header in last night's partido against the despised Real Madrid; and whether the family apartment in the pueblo will be available for next weekend. Time is elastic in Spain.

Although change is not welcome, improvisation is. It's why you can have a great meal from a near-empty refrigerator, why the door knob always comes off in your hand over and over again, and why you'll rarely get an RSVP until the last minute, if at all. It's a great way of living and cooking.

All of this ancient gri-gri voodoo translates into many things. A patriarchal culture that is actually created and sustained by matriarchs. Dry cleaners that close for three hours in the middle of the day, never mind that everybody else is out and about during the siesta, eating, napping, and looking for an open dry cleaner. Drinking lots of tiny beers rather than one big one because God might not notice. There is this intangible connection between sin, redemption, *albóndigas*, socialists, and fascists. Spain is a perpetual motion teeter-totter, always swinging between two extreme points. Sol and sombra. Anarchy and fascism. Fiesta and famine. Stuffy and old fashioned and informality in everything. Isn't this contradictory? Of course it is. It's Iberia. It's the Mediterranean.

Consider how those who inhabit the peninsula eat. They might put out the fancy china and glassware; they might shell out for eighty euro a kilo *jamon*, or lay down big time for a few *percebres* (barnacles!), the harvesting of which every year takes the life of many *percerberos*; or spend all day stuffing *canalons*. Regardless, they are still going to eat with their hands, steal food off of fellow diners' plates, eat directly off the serving platter, use their tongues to get deep into inaccessible crustacean crevices, and wash everything down with an astounding amount of *vino tinto*, *cava*, *cerveza*, *vermut*, *chupitos de aguardiente*, *orujo*, *pacharan*, *ratafia*, or Baileys served in anything from a Lalique flute to a repurposed Nocilla jar.

I'm not sure where this style of eating came from. Perhaps from their collective agrarian past; or perhaps due to the fact that even Juan Carlos, the abdicated King, eats ham with his bare hands (he also shot elephants while simultaneously heading up the World Wildlife Federation, but that's another story). Consider how the Iberian tradition of digging into a communal platter of migas so closely mirrors how the people on the other side of the Mediterranean eat their tagine and couscous. Regardless of the history, for me this earthy kind of eating is right in the pocket; it's neither overly fussy nor too reverential (as is often the case in the bordering country to the north). But neither does it require inhaling a double down chicken sandwich made out of a fried and breaded chicken breast sandwiched between two more fried and breaded chicken breasts, accompanied by a sixty-four ounce maxi bucket of Mountain Dew, while en route in a Humvee to watch "Iron Man gets a Hang Nail" at the Mega-mega-plex. *"Oye Paco*, you gonna eat that barnacle?"

POSTRES

MANZANAS al HORNO

BAKED APPLES. WHAT COULD BE MORE SIMPLE? TAKE APPLES. BAKE APPLES. EAT BAKED APPLES.

Class, as we have learned, simple is, more often than not, better than complicated. And, as has been mentioned many times before, this means the quality of the ingredients matter, so try to find some really exceptional apples. Heirlooms? Sure, just make sure they are firm and on the tart side. Granny Smith's work just fine too, as does a quality golden if your flavor profile skews to the sweet side. Hey, try a few types and compare.

4   apples (figure 1 apple per person)

1   teaspoon of brown sugar per apple

1   hearty pour of brandy, cognac, dark rum or Cointreau or Grand Marnier per apple. You may, if you wish, do as they do at Pinotxo, and use a cocktail that is equal parts brandy, rum and Cointreau.

1   cup of water

1   Preheat oven to 180° C/350° F.

2   Making sure to leave the bottom of the apples intact, core the apples with an apple corer. Imagine that you are making a little apple cup… or more accurately a little apple shot glass. If you wish, you may do as they do at the bar and cut off the top of the apple core and save it as a little hat.

3   Place the apples in a baking dish, low casserole or a cazuela. Add the water to the pan.

4   Load the brown sugar into each apple and then follow with the alcohol. If you have saved the little apple hat, cover the hole with it.

5   Place in oven and bake for 40 minutes to one hour. Every once in a while check for doneness with a fork. When they are soft, they are done.

6   As a variation you could add a cinnamon stick to each apple, but then sadly, you will have to lose the hat.

CROISSANT AZUCARADO

1. Take one high quality croissant.
2. Take one hot plancha (griddle or pan).
3. Take a hearty handful of sugar.
4. Place the sugar on the plancha.
5. Let the sugar heat up and begin to melt.
6. Take the croissant and, with its top facing down into the now partially molten sugar, rub it 'round and 'round until the sugar is caramelized and stuck to the inverted pastry. Flip it over, put it on a plate and violà… dessert is served.

Let's face it. Pinotxo is not the place to grab a piece of cheesecake, a skinny latte "**DOPPIO MACCHIATO DOPPIO DOPPIO**", pop open your macbook air, and spend the afternoon working on your screenplay. It's an insanely busy bar with a hovering mass of humanity that's sometimes six deep. For such a popular and bustling destination the dessert menu is a bit limited. But like everything else, what they do, they do well, including impromptu lunchtime *postres*.

Take this brilliant and simple recipe that has its origins in Catalan frugality and aversion to waste. What to do with the rare, occasional morning's leftover pastries? Since they definitely won't be returning for a second day, they can be either eaten as is, thrown out, or transformed into another dish… say a quick, delicious, and unique dessert for the lunchtime crowd.

The stars are fading into the dawn sky. La luna is floating above Montjuïc and Calatrava's undoubtedly "plagued by cost overruns" communication tower for the 1992 Olympics. The sun is just peeking over the lip of the Mediterranean. The shrieking swallows have begun dive bombing insects for breakfast. I try to start my day up here on the roof.

Since the Pinotxo adventure began, I often think about the fact that Jordi and Juanito are pulling up the *persiana* and making the first rounds of *cafés con leche* while I am either still in bed or drinking my coffee, watching dronelike black birds eat bugs, and thinking about my good fortune.

I have been in Spain for fifteen years. My Spanish still sucks. My Catalan is nonexistent. Except for a few months in the USA, my daughter has spent her whole life here; and this year begins her final two years of pre-college studies. Yes, the weather's great, the food's terrific, the women are beautiful and grounded, and if need be can probably rebuild your carburetor. In the space of a few hours you can take a metro to the sea and a train to the mountains, but for me it really boils down to one thing; I feel at home here. I truly love the people. Sure Barcelona is insanely loud (those damn two cycle 50cc "motos"), everybody talks at the same time, there is only a small, but passionate live music scene, the gallery world is not exactly cutting edge, and the Catalan separatist movement is what it is, but for me it's the best place in the world. It is, for a very extended moment, my home. Gràcies, a tots.

ROBIN WILLIS

PHOTO *credits*

All photos by Becky Lawton except:

Cover photo by Robin Willis

Photo on page 12 by David Reamer

Photo on page 14 by Josep Echaburu

Photo on page 49 by Mario Scattoloni

Photos on pages 26, 32, 37, 63, 64, 65 and
Espanyol coat of arms on page 38 by Robin Willis

On page 22, clockwise from top; photos 1, 2 and 4
by Mario Scattoloni and 3 by Robin Willis

On page 25, clockwise from top left; photos 1, 3, 4
and 5 by Robin Willis and 2 by Mario Scattoloni

On page 29, all photos by Robin Willis except for
correfocs by Mario Scattoloni

Photo on page 55 by Robin Willis